The
BOLD
Business
Book

**A strategy guide to start, run and love
your BOLD business.**

by James Kademan

Cover Illustration Copyright © 2017
Cover design by Pixelstudio
Book design and production by James Kademan
Edited by RescueDesk Virtual Assistants, Trisha Alcisto and Tania Therien
Author photograph by Beth Skogen
Library of Congress Control Number: 2017916829
Kademan, James, 1977-
The Bold Business Book: A Strategy Guide to Start, Run and Love Your Bold Business / James Kademan
ISBN 9780999025840 softcover
ISBN 9780999025857 ebook
ISBN 9780999025864 hardcover
ISBN 9780999025871 audiobook
Printed in the United States of America

To my dearest Robyn for tolerating me, my happiest Max for reminding me, and my kindest Kirby for the constant advice given with only a look.

> # "Fortuna audaces iuvat
> -Latin Proverb"

Fortune favors the bold.

"Only the meek get pinched. The bold survive."

-Ferris Bueller, *Ferris Bueller's Day Off*

Table of Contents

Introduction

Are you ready to be bold? Readers like you who design their own world and navigate their way in it are an inspiration to myself and others. I'm proud to be a writer and hoping I can offer you some guidance as you work towards leaving your own mark on the world. This book is intended to accomplish three things:

1) Get you motivated to make the progress your business needs.
2) Give you tools to make the progress your business needs.
3) Be enjoyable enough to succeed at numbers 1 & 2.

The topics brought to light in this book are for you to read, consider, and decide if they apply to you and your business. I've done my best to share my take on the challenges that lead to hard-earned, experience-based insight. But every person—and I mean every person—has their own unique view of the world and an experience to match. You may find yourself either nodding in agreement or vigorously shaking your head as I lead you along the path I took and tell you about those taken by others. But this is one of the things I find so fascinating about business: When it comes to achieving business goals, there are as many pathways as there are people.

You may be wondering why I decided to write this book,

and perhaps even what I mean by Bold Business. Bold can certainly be defined a number of different ways—in this book, it is defined as acknowledging any fear and moving forward to achieve your goals regardless of what may come. With or without all of the information, the bold check their gut and move accordingly. Sometimes all it takes to be bold is to be the one that seizes an opportunity.

Think of someone you consider bold. Someone that exemplifies the definition of boldness as a personality trait. You know there are people who respect, admire, and appreciate them. But they've also got some haters. You need haters. Without them you're clearly not being noticed.

It's been said that if you want to make an omelette, you need to break some eggs. If you want your actions to be bold actions, you're going to need a new frame of mind, one that will make you an unstoppable force. Your job is to use that powerful force for good and to weather some unexpected consequences. Be prepared to make a few enemies as you attract a growing crowd of admirers.

During the course of writing The Bold Business Book, I've met with hundreds of business owners from a broad spectrum of industries. Each has a story and wisdom to share. Where the value lies is in their real-world experience, which you can use as a guide to maneuver through the ups and downs of business ownership and learn not only how to survive, but to thrive.

You'll get to know these experienced contributors throughout the book. They've supplied how-to's as well as do's and don'ts for everything—from finding the right merchant provider for accepting credit card payments to purchasing advertising without wasting money. Their insights are distributed throughout the book. They have graciously allowed me to include their contact information should you need more help in their areas of expertise.

Finally, I love hearing from business owners. Every time I meet with an entrepreneur, we talk for far longer than originally planned. The journey of business ownership is challenging, risky, and time-consuming, and the stories I hear are incredible. The rewards are truly limitless with the right mindset.

I hope I get to meet you someday and learn from what you have to share. Congrats on taking the leap to start and grow your own business. If you feel inclined, and I hope you do, please send your business stories to james@drawincustomers.com.

 Lessons Learned: Decide and Act

Throughout this book you will see some Lessons Learned boxes. These are brief summaries of the lesson to be learned in the corresponding narrative. Your first lesson is to decide if you will be bold and if you will act on that decision. Seriously, decide to keep reading and be sure to take action on what you learn.

Chapter 1

**More time, more money, more fun.
You got this.**

> **"**
> *One day our life will flash before our eyes.
> Make sure it is worth watching.*
> -Gerard Way
> **"**

The traffic is thick on a Friday afternoon. I was cruising with my family up the highway to spend time with some extended family on a lake. I was driving my wife's Toyota Prius C. If you aren't familiar with a Prius C, it's essentially the less manly, though less conspicuous, version of a normal Prius. We were in some thicker traffic, and a Ferrari casually rolled past us. The Ferrari's license plate read: BOSSMAN.

"Awesome," I said.

"Whatever," my wife replied with a well-timed eye roll.

This led to a heated discussion over what makes a good car and an acceptable license plate. What I knew was that I was driving my wife's Prius C, and that guy was driving a Ferrari. He could be having a worse conversation and would still be having more fun.

Our dispute ultimately landed on the license plate. It did not say, WORKER B, HRD WRKR, or TRST FND. It read BOSSMAN, presumably because this person was a boss in the business sense, and a little ego spilled onto his car. After all, isn't a cool car one of the things people use to judge success? You could argue all day about the merits of BOSSMAN as a license plate. For all we know, the guy has 50 employees that roll in cars that cost twice as much as his.

I tell you this because I want to be that guy. But, the truth is, I didn't always. There was a time when I would have seen that car and made a joke about him being a prick or snubbed my nose at the waste of funds on such a beautiful car that no one in the world should have. Except me. And maybe a few friends.

I was jealous of the financial success of people I had never met. How often do you find yourself judging people for accomplishments that you are trying to achieve? Is it possible to think that you may be your own worst enemy? You bet it is. What will you do to hold yourself back?

The answer is just about anything, most of which you won't even notice. Tell me again about your excuses to not make those phone calls, send those emails, set the meetings you need, or finish up that project. Obstacles are often created by ourselves to prevent us from achieving the success we want.

The simple solution is to love the Ferrari. Don't be jealous of the Ferrari. Look forward to obnoxious insurance premiums and a few speeding tickets. More than that, be proud of the person rolling in that car. Treat them like Chevy Chase treated Christie Brinkley in National Lampoon's Vacation movie when she passed him in her Ferrari. Learn from them, respect them, and keep giving yourself something to strive for.

When you roll up in your Ferrari (or your version of the Ferrari), I want you to entertain the observers and let them know you look forward to seeing them driving an even better car one day. Your job as a successful person is to bring more success into this world. That is what bold business is all about.

> " *"Everyone pities the weak.*
> *Jealousy you have to earn"*
> -Arnold Schwarzenegger "

Why, Why, Why

If I were to ask you why you do what you do in your business and in life, you'd probably have an answer. Perhaps it's safe to say that, as you ponder this question, you're asking yourself, "Why do I do what I do?" Seriously—what reason do you have for starting a business? Why do you operate the way you do? I mean really, is it for the potential to make money? Is it for the possibility of freedom? Is it because the thought of waking up each day to work for someone else eats at your soul? Or do you just want to see your business idea come to life? Whatever it may be, clearly defining your reasons for going down the twisting road of entrepreneurship will help you succeed.

Once you've that figured out, it'll be time to advance your business. In order to do that, it will help to have some tools, tools that many business owners never fully utilize or realize they have. These tools include knowledge, experience, contacts, persistence, patience and perhaps a few understanding friends. This book will help you by offering some additional tools as well as help you discover tools you didn't even know you had.

The Bold Business Book offers insight to help you reach three things for you and your business: more time, more money, and more fun. We all want these three things to some degree as we progress through life and business.

So let's return to our question. Why do you do what you do? You are doing what you do for a feeling. That's it. Everything you do is so you can experience a feeling. Typically, we're after positive feelings. Starting a business should feel good. Much like eating cake, getting naked or chilling with friends. Maybe all three together. Running your business should feel just as good.

 Lessons Learned: Define Your Reason

> Let me be clear on this whole 'feeling' thing. You need a more in-depth answer than "a desire for a feeling of happiness." Go deeper, strive to uncover what is inside of you that is calling you on this path. Something along the lines of a mission statement, such as, "The purpose of my life is to be kick-ass, helpful, enjoy making people smile, and do the best I can for myself and others."

The feelings you may initially feel as a result of pursuing your goals may actually be negative, though not intentional or often necessary. The feelings I'm speaking of are the feelings which may be negative for a moment such as: disgust, overwhelm, frustration and fear. However, they are justified by the end feeling of gratification as you achieve your underlying goal. To act in a bold manner means to move beyond the moment with your mind set on what you are after and why you are after it.

> "Everyone is so offended by the mindset it takes to be the best in the world."
> -Ronda Rousey

Polishing a Turd

I owned a 1979 Chevy Malibu station wagon for almost 17 years. It was my first car, and I loved that thing. A few years ago, I decided to fix up that beautiful cruiser. I gave it a smooth paint job—a metallic midnight blue that sparkled and shined with so much depth it was like you were staring into a still lake at dawn. But it still had a lethargic 305-cubic-inch engine. It was a V8 rated at 145 horsepower. To put that into perspective, a 2016 Honda

Civic puts out 158 horsepower from a 91-cubic-inch engine and weighs about 500 pounds less. That means a third of the engine size and more power to boot. So this hotrod would get schooled at stoplight drags by a base-model economy car. To say something needed to change was like saying water is wet.

All I needed was to install a new engine—it would take some knuckle skin to make its way between the fenders, but it would offer the best of everything: a newer mechanical beast with more power while being easier on the environment.

So I swapped in the fancy engine. I worked on getting everything set up just the way I wanted. It took me three to four years. Then the time came for me to start using the car. I enjoyed the new power, but I started noticing little noises, things that seem to plague every project car. I had to drive and decipher those audible clues at the same time. What was that little pinging noise? Oh, that was the exhaust hanger. Need to adjust that a bit. These types of things slip your notice when a car is sitting still, so driving and deciphering became a way of life with the newly minted "Malibeast."

One day, I was waiting at a stoplight. It was a gorgeous morning of bright skies and clear roads. As the light turned green, I released the brake and feathered the throttle. As I accelerated, the Malibeast came to life quicker and smoother than anticipated—it was like I hit the afterburners on a jet.

I didn't build this car to stay with traffic, I wanted to define it, so I hit the gas. Midway up the block, as my engine was singing that sweet American-muscle sound, my car upshifted. After that small interruption of power to the tires while the gears changed, power was reapplied to the wheels, and the tires broke loose; on dry pavement and at 60 miles per hour, the Malibeast chirped its tires.

The chirp was probably inaudible to anyone else—I was light years ahead of the crowd and a city is a noisy place in the morning. But I was keenly aware as the tires briefly lost traction. The feeling I had in that moment was why I had put years of time,

8

money, and effort into that car—it was all just for that split second reward. The smile I had as the goosebumps of success covered my body revealed that it was all worth it.

Now, I like cars, so a feeling of success and insurmountable joy came after my personal success with the Malibeast. You may like something else. You may be after a different feeling. Are you taking the actions you need to take to achieve the feelings you desire? Or are you falling into the trap of comfortable mediocrity?

Imagine if you had a defined purpose, or mission statement that organized itself around the feelings you want. Would you sit around watching another rerun or would you go take some action?

What has Worked for You

If you currently have a business, what impresses you about it? What parts of your business help bring out the positive, encouraging, motivational feelings you want? What did you do to make those things happen? Write down five actions you took that helped you achieve these feelings:

_____

_____

_____

_____

_____

Reflect on these five actions. How did these actions come about? Were they coincidental? Did you have to struggle to achieve them? Were you even aware before you wrote them down that they were part of what pushed your business forward?

The point of this exercise is to help you see that your life is defined by many choices, often without you even being conscious of them.

In the case of the Malibeast, I went through a lot for barely more than a moment's gratification. After the morning her tires chirped, I was walking on clouds remembering what I had accomplished. I also felt a huge energy rush, like I could run faster than a jet right before takeoff. But what if I didn't have to go through all of that work to achieve that elevated feeling? What if I could simply choose to feel that way? I realized that I could in fact do this, and I sold the Malibeast the following year.

Through this epiphany I came to discover more insights, and also more questions. If I can choose to have certain feelings like those chirping tires gave me when I wanted, then could I also choose to have higher energy levels when I needed them?

How many people grab coffee in the morning to energize themselves? What's crazy about this is that we already have the tools within us to get moving, but we've trained our minds to depend on outside help. Some of that outside help, such as coffee, TV, sugar, or other vices of various repute may get you going. But have you ever thought about what would happen if you simply trained your mind to get the feelings you need from your vice without your vice?

> "My life is a road, man. I need to keep moving."
> -Matthew McConaughey

You've Got the Power

I want to be clear: I'm not here to preach to you about "bad" vices. I think coffee tastes pretty good with loads of sugar and cream. What I am suggesting is that you consider finding suitable alternatives within yourself for that kick, that energy. You do this so that when you find yourself feeling down or not ready to take on a new challenge, you're able to get yourself going with zero external stimulus in an instant.

You've seen the images of Buddhist monks sitting calmly while they're on fire in protest against political persecution. Or think of the hunger strikes that others have endured. Forget why they do this for a moment, think of the how. Did that flaming monk feel like he needed to hit Starbuck's before he grabbed a match? His motivation came entirely from within.

You may believe these people are just crazy, but you'd be missing the point. The lesson to take away is what these folks were able to motivate themselves to do with nothing more than their own decisions. You can, too. That is to say, your mind and their mind, we can agree, are equal in power and capability. Maybe you don't want to light yourself on fire in political protest, but I bet you could make some sales calls instead, couldn't you? They want social justice; you want to grow your business. The mind that most people are given at birth is equal to most everyone else's. We ourselves limit the possibilities of what we can achieve either through our beliefs or our values.

The human mind has the power and capability to allow us to go through intense pain when motivated—all pain and pleasure happens in our minds. Luckily for us, a mind this powerful sits between our ears.

And what if you could harness that power and train your mind to use that power to drive you forward?

> **"I have no fear of losing my life. If I have to save a koala or a crocodile or a kangaroo or a snake, mate, I will save it."**
> -Steve Irwin

If I were to see you in the morning and said a cheery hello before you've had your coffee, how would you react? Maybe not so great. Now imagine I kicked you in the shin instead of saying hello. Do you have to find the energy to respond or do you naturally power up? Imagine instead that I just handed you a bag of money, telling you it's yours as long as you smile the rest of the day. Are you able to muster up a smile, or do you truly need to hit the coffee maker first?

Many people, caffeine addicted or not, can react when

11

provoked in a way they didn't realize they could. The challenge, of course, is to tap into that energy without getting kicked in the shin. This example illustrates that we have the power to be and do whatever we want, we've simply trained ourselves not to. We have been seduced by the allure of mediocrity. If you've listened to that siren song too much, let's change that right now.

 Lessons Learned: Find the Motivation

Finding what motivates you goes a bit beyond the whole "why" thing. Everyone has a reason or multiple reasons to do what they do. How many can get the energy and the drive to get up and act on those reasons with little thought? Learn to power yourself with the physiology and focus that will get you going and keep you moving. Emotion will lead to motion.

You Got This

I want you to practice something with me. This will start out a bit weird, but bear with me: Your level of kick-ass is about to go all the way to Level 11. I want you to say the words, "I Got This!" out loud. If you're in a place where this will result in embarrassment, say them in your head. Just promise me that at some point in the next week, you will say, "I Got This!" at least ten times out loud.

> "Note to self: If you were able to believe in Santa Claus for 8 years, you can believe in yourself for 5 seconds. You got this."
>
> -Rebel Circus

Now I want you to think of a time when you were surprisingly successful. Maybe you won, achieving what you were going for even when you weren't sure you could. Or maybe you were much younger, and you received an award for something you didn't even know you could do, but you found a way and broke through. At that moment you defined success.

Think of that moment and at the peak of satisfaction, I want you to yell out, "I Got This!"

Again, "I Got This!"
Again, "I Got This!"

Again, "I Got This!"

Now this time I want you to stress the word "I." As in, "**I** Got This!"

Again, "**I** Got This!"

Again, "**I** Got This!"

Again, "**I** Got This!"

Now this time I want you to stress the word "Got." As in, "I **Got** This!"

Again, "I **Got** This!"

Again, "I **Got** This!"

Again, "I **Got** This!"

I know you can see where this is going. When you stress the word, "This," I want you to feel the word "this" as defining everything you have ever wanted to conquer. Stand up, or if you are in your car, straighten up.

Punch your right hand into your left palm and shout out, "I Got **This!**"

13

Punch your hand again into your palm and shout out, "I Got **This!**"

Punch your hand again into your palm and shout out, "I Got **This!**"

Now stand tall, look around, and feel that you can take on any challenge. When someone tells you that you can't, that you don't have the guts, the drive, the knowledge or the capabilities, what are you going to say?

"I Got This!"

When you feel that energy and intensity streaming through your body, flowing through every vein and triggering all the right synapses in your brain, when you feel this rush of dominating energy, you will understand that you are an unstoppable force. As you take a deep breath and feel the oxygen feed that energy that grows in intensity, you'll feel lighter. You will be smarter. You will be stronger. You will have clarity about what needs to be done.

Stand tall, raise your arms up in the air, and feel the energy pulsing through you, around you, and feel the energy waiting for a command from you. Listen as it whistles past you, around you, and through you. What color is this energy? How bright is it? Is it warm or cool? Are you calm and accepting of this energy?

This energy is available to you at any time, day or night, any season, any time, any place. You carry it with you, and it only helps you. Your only job is to guide it into the places you need it.

Shout one last time and feel the pulsing of the energy as you punch your right hand into your left fist three times with each syllable and announce boldly, "I Got This!"

Now I want you to bring yourself back to where you were. Where was your body ten minutes ago? Were you sitting casually? Maybe a little slouched? Recall what you felt ten minutes ago. How much energy did you have? Compare that with what you felt a minute ago. Which do you prefer? What can you do to bring back that vibrant energy that gives you access to the energy needed to accomplish what moments ago you thought was impossible? Do it now. You got this.

Lessons Learned: It's OK to be Awesome

In Ben Franklin's autobiography, he noted that many people had requested that he write his own biography. He included a four-page letter from his friend Benjamin Vaughan telling him that he needs to write his biography and outlining why. Not an email or a text, but a handwritten, four-page letter. That's how you know you are awesome. You can be that awesome, and I wish you the best in achieving that level of bold success.

What Was That

For some, what I've just suggested may feel like an unorthodox approach to tapping into the reserves of strength and passion that each of us possesses. But for others, the exercise is a trusted resource they know they can turn to again and again until "I Got This!" becomes more than a mantra.

What do you risk by giving it a try, alone, in private place where no one can hear or see you? Humor me for a moment and just think about what would happen if you did it, and it worked.

> *"Your dream doesn't have an expiration date. Take a deep breath and try again."*
> -KT Witten

A Warning

I want to caution you regarding the content of this book. You see, this is a bold business book, which means we can't just tiptoe around the challenges for business owners. We can't pretend that starting, owning, and running a business is all moonbeams and rainbows. Business is tough. And like most tough things, we respect and appreciate them. Sometimes we even jump in and join them.

Tough is what we live for as business owners. If you are in business, you'd better be tough and be proud of it.

In this book, you'll be presented with some challenges. You'll read about some obstacles and traps that most business owners at some point must overcome or resist. You'll learn that the battle that is your business is really just inside your head. The good news is, you're reading this to overcome and succeed.

> *"Take a deep breath, pick yourself up, dust yourself off, and start all over again."*
> -Frank Sinatra, *Pick Yourself Up*

Chapter 2

This isn't really all about you, is it?

> ❝
> *"To make it in life, you and your wife need to be in the same business. That has been my problem all along. My wives didn't know what I was doing. I would come back home from the road to a stranger. That's no good."*
> ❞
> -James Brown

Now that you know how to feel energized and are aware that I may ask you to do a few crazy things throughout this book, let's keep going.

I started my first business in 2006. I crunched all the numbers, determined what it would take to succeed, calculated how much cash I could make, and mapped out the challenges I thought I'd be up against. For all the planning, prep work, and paper I powered through, I missed one small piece: I gave zero fucks about what my wife was thinking.

She didn't challenge me too much in general, but in all honesty, I didn't think it really mattered. I knew one of two things would happen: I was either going to be successful as a business owner or just roll back and get a normal job. End of story. As it turns out, not paying attention to my wife's concerns was a pretty big misstep. Ignoring your family is a terrible way to start a business and a fantastic way to end a marriage. If I were a divorce lawyer, I would hang around banks looking for budding entrepreneurs getting loans. I'd stand outside and hand out my card. See you in six months, my friend.

It's not that I didn't care about my wife's feelings; it just didn't occur to me that her feelings were relevant. It's like the clouds overhead—unless it rains, I assume they're fine. Starting a business is tough. It's painful and challenging. Shouldn't your spouse just be proud of everything you're creating?

Hindsight tells a much different story. When you start a business, your spouse, your family, and the people closest to you will be affected. When I was in the process of starting my business, I remember laying in bed next to my wife brainstorming with her all of the options for what business I could start. Do I buy a franchise restaurant? Get into screen printing? Maybe fire up my old graphic design skills? The list was long. Conversations like that, I learned later, scared the hell out of my wife.

The funny thing is … well … it really wasn't funny. The enlightening thing, then, is that my wife's perception of me starting a business, and then starting another, and constantly being out networking and schmoozing with other business owners took a toll on our marriage. The challenges I faced in business were immediate and apparent; the challenges my business caused in my relationship didn't smack me in the face until years after it had started. I still shake my head at my own lack of insight.

This isn't really all about you, is it?

> *"Sometimes you just have to take a step back and realize what's important in your life, what you can live with, but more importantly, what you can't live without."*
> -Lauren Conrad

It seems silly doesn't it? How could anyone not understand their relationship is cracking under the pressure of starting a business? But many entrepreneurs seem to overlook things like this. After all, we're bulldozers. Does a bulldozer care if it runs over a flower? All the bulldozer knows is that a path needs to be cleared. Another flower will grow. Bulldozers don't pause because it would take too much power to start up again. Not to mention, a pause leaves a wrinkle, a bump in the dirt that interrupts the flow. Bulldozers do not stop for flowers because bulldozers cannot see the flowers in front of them.

Lessons Learned: When Your What and Your Why Get in the Way of Your Who.

I was brutal in my disregard for my family's sacrifices when starting a business. At the time, I naively thought I was the one doing all the sacrificing, but in reality, what was I really sacrificing if I knew that I would be successful? I was sacrificing time with my family without even asking permission.

Before you start a business, take inventory of your relationships. You might have a girlfriend or boyfriend, maybe a spouse, maybe some kids, probably some friends. The time you have available for them will change after you launch a business. Reflect on what it will mean to those relationships when you go off on your own.

The same exercise is useful even if you have been in business for years. Just like counting the inventory taking up space on your shelves, it helps to count your relationships. Note that more does not necessarily equal better. Quality is of greater concern than quantity.

Once you've taken inventory of your relationships, project what might happen to these relationships after you start your business. Some relationships will tolerate much more than others. You may find it acceptable to lose or to see some relationships weakened. Others you have worked your entire life for, so they mean the most. Keep in mind that I am in no way telling you not to start a business just because someone you are close to told you not to. Maintaining the relationships with those you are close to may prove challenging.

> "You want to know who your friends are? Start your own business and ask for their support."
> -Steve Jobs

The main challenge for a BOLD business owner is to understand that your business isn't all about you. It is about your family, your employees, your customers, and society as a whole. Are you making the world a better place by doing what you are doing?

I struggled with that for years. I was doing all the work getting my business going—struggling to find customers, dealing with vendors and suppliers, and chatting up people who were more artificial than plastic Christmas trees. I was learning how to read people beyond what they were saying and to understand their point of view. All of this was making me a much better business person while, at the same time, draining the life out of my marriage. I was spending so much time in, on, and around my business that I failed to spend time with the people I was doing it for. I bled business. It was all that I truly enjoyed. It consumed me. I just wanted more. This can be a disheartening thing to realize and a frustrating challenge to overcome.

Like you, I am a bulldozer. When I realized my relationship

was getting rocky, I kept on pushing. My go-to solution for just about any challenge is to simply give it more throttle. I put the hustle into my business to a fault. That, as you can imagine, didn't do anything to help. Eventually (and thankfully) I got smart and figured it out.

Real World Experience from The Spouse
My wife

When my husband told me he was going to start a business, I freaked out.

I hadn't ever known anyone who owned a business. In my experience, everyone put in their hours and got a paycheck. Owning a business was stepping pretty far into the unknown, and I was scared. "What would happen if..." filled my mind and, as I look back on it, I think my husband took each one of those questions and replaced it with "I don't think you'll be able to make it." This made for a very stressful time in our marriage. Soon, I stopped asking and just started panicking on my own. The few times we did talk about it, it ended in a fight.

But, if I could go back in time, I'd do things a bit differently during the planning and start-up phase of his business:

I'd start by saying, "I trust you and know you will do amazing things." While I have tremendous faith in my husband, I let my fears get the better of me and I didn't encourage him enough. If I could redo it all, I would have kept saying it because, at the end of the day, I believe it to be true. It would have helped him and me. All I focused on were my fears, giving my fear all the power.

I'd ask to be included during the set-up. I think part of

my freak-outs were that I didn't know everything he had been thinking about and doing to make sure the business would be a success. I heard some of the frustrations, but didn't really know about the things that went well.

We'd talk about money. Money is a scary thing to talk about for a lot of couples, and it was my biggest fear. It would have helped to have grown-up discussions about how much money he had, how much he would potentially make, and what we could do if things got tough.

I'd ask for acknowledgement of my feelings. My husband is a fixer so, as a result, he would try to "fix" the fears I shared with him. I didn't need them fixed; I just needed him to say he understood why it was scary.

I'd remind him that our time together is important. As he started his business, our time revolved around his work. On our way out to dinner, we'd have to stop to drop off a package or pick something up. While in the car headed for a weekend out of town, I'd have to hop online to order something. I often felt like a second thought. I don't mind it during the work day, but it was spilling over into our personal lives way too much.

Ten years into being a business owner's wife, I'm not as scared. We've taken time to do the things we should have at the beginning, and I'm excited to see and be part of his next successful adventure. If you are getting ready to take the leap, remember there is someone else who will be impacted. Hopefully you can learn from what I wish I'd done and make that leap a little smoother!

Time > Money

The true change came after I read Timothy Ferriss' *The Four-Hour Workweek*. In it, Ferriss challenged the notion that you need to work hard to achieve success. It was a huge paradigm shift to read and understand what he meant. It spoke of the "new rich," those who value free time and experiences as much as they value money. What good is money if you don't have time to enjoy it? Or even more importantly, have people to share that time and money with?

All this talk of personal relationships might seem a bit sappy. But consider how challenging it was for you to get the family you wanted in the first place. Relationships take work to maintain and even more work to mold into the relationships you want.

> *"A friendship founded on business is better than a business founded on friendship."*
> -John D. Rockefeller

You need to go after your relationships the same way you go after your BOLD business. You need to be the best you can be and push yourself to be better than you thought possible. The rewards for both go beyond what you now consider acceptable. It's worth taking on the challenge of keeping you, your family, and your business well balanced and happy. It's also achievable, despite what others may have you believe.

This also goes in the relationships you cultivate as you grow your business. Beyond your family, you will add people to your tribe from all walks of life. Your customers, vendors, employees, and even all the salespeople hustling alongside you to sell the latest and greatest whatever.

I can't emphasize the importance of your network enough; it's a great source of power. I never could have started my businesses as easily as I did without the networks I've built over the years. These are the people you'll turn to for advice, have a drink with, celebrate victories with, and learn from.

Of all of the people you meet, there are a few who need to be taken care of more than others. For example, never, under any circumstance, piss off the UPS, FedEX, or USPS person. Ever.

There will be times you need that delivery person to go the extra ten feet for you or leave a package for you while you stepped out to get lunch. Annoy your delivery person at your business's peril. Your vendors will come and go and customers may come and go.

Your delivery people are the lifeblood of motion in your business. This goes for every type of business—retail stores, restaurants, professional services, trades businesses, and everything in between. Sooner or later, you will have something shipped to you.

> "I have made some of the best friends that I've got in this business."
> -Kate Moss

People are Awesome

After more than a decade of being my own boss, one of the greatest insights I've discovered in meeting people from all over my little corner of the world is how the landscape is constantly evolving. People I have known for years change jobs annually; salespeople who hounded me for years suddenly turn 180 degrees and now work in unrelated careers; people have gotten cancer, passed away, had kids, gotten divorced, and started other businesses. It's amazing how the people around you change, and how this knowledge changes your view of the business landscape.

What this means is that you are not the only butterfly, my friend. Just about every business owner around you is hustling and changing in one way or another. You are there to help them just as much, if not more, than they are there to help you. Treat people like tools in your toolbox; one day you may find that you have a screw to turn and can't find a screwdriver anywhere. That may sound odd, but I really love my tools.

This isn't really all about you, is it?

> *"How many people you bless is how you measure success."*
>
> -Rick Ross

The great part about having all of these business relationships is the wonderful camaraderie and glorious understanding of perilous challenges. If I go home and tell my wife I lost a deal, she reconsiders the mortgage, starts planning a garage sale, switches to cheap dog food, and wonders why she married a fool who can't close a sale. If I tell a business friend I lost a sale, we usually laugh about it because my friend probably knows the cheap SOB who didn't buy from me. We know that if someone doesn't buy, someone else will. Customers come and go. Nothing lasts forever.

I have found that my business friends are just as close, if not closer, than my other friends. My non-business-owning friends are great people. But, with entrepreneur friends, it's a little different; they understand the zone. It all comes down to what you chat about and what you do during your fun times.

Most of my non-business-owner friends chat about TV shows or movies or sports or cars or current events. My work-related friends may talk a bit about that stuff, but then we move straight back into business. We all sleep, eat, and breathe the work we do. Business people are never off. Much like new parents on a rare date without their children, the conversation often turns back towards the kids. This is despite the often desperate attempts to avoid the topic.

If you are a business owner, I am certain you understand this. If you will be starting your venture soon, this will creep up on you before you can say, "What hobbies?"

> ❝
> *"Lots of people want to ride with you on the limo, but what you want is someone who will ride the bus with you when the limo breaks down."*
> ❞
> -Oprah Winfrey

Never Off

A few years ago, my wife and I went to Florida for the first real vacation we had had since our wedding. I had started my receptionist business by then, so I knew my phone was being answered, and my employees assured me everything would still be around when I returned.

As we were checking into our hotel, the printer stopped working for the front desk person. I came around the counter and fixed the thing with my pen. Since one of my companies was in printer repair, I gave the clerk my card and told her that if they expanded into Wisconsin, I could help them more often. As we were talking, the phone started to ring and the clerk assured us voicemail would grab it. I then gave her the card for our receptionist business, and told her we could answer their overflow calls too. When you have a business, you are never off.

> ❝
> *"The successful business executive can handle challenges and solve problems at a remarkable clip."*
> ❞
> -Zig Ziglar

Love the Haters

One thing you need to remember is that you will meet people who do not want you to succeed. To them, your success means that they are not successful. Some people will see a person driving a Ferrari and think terrible things about them. Exactly like I used to do. They'll think, "That BOSSMAN Ferrari driver could have solved world hunger, made peace in every nation, and cured cancer. Instead he chose to buy a fancy car. What a jerk."

Those same people then go back to watching cable TV in their name-brand shoes. Fancy, but not too fancy, right? Who is to say what is acceptable for you to have as trinkets of your success? Not me, my friend. Abundance is everywhere.

> "A tough lesson in life is that one has to learn that not everybody wishes you well."
> -Dan Rather

Chapter 3

" *"I've missed more than 9000 shots in my career. I've lost almost 300 games. 26 times, I've been trusted to take the game winning shot and missed. I've failed over and over and over again in my life. And that is why I succeed."*

"   -Michael Jordan

In 1900, Albert Einstein graduated with a degree in physics. In 1905, as a young physicist, he published four papers including the first exploration of the theory of special relativity. These papers detailed theories that had yet to be proven. A solar eclipse was needed to illustrate the light of outlying stars bending around the sun. The chance to photograph just such an event took place in 1914.

Erwin Finlay-Freundlich, William Wallace Campbell and their respective teams took on the challenge of proving or disproving Einstein. Unfortunately, the location from which to view this solar eclipse was in Russia, which was a challenge because of Germany's declaration of war on Russia. Finlay-Freundlich and his assistants, who were German nationals, were captured as POWs in Russia, and their equipment was seized. Although Campbell, an American, was able to keep the process moving, cloud cover obscured the eclipse making the entire trip fruitless. However, failure commonly leads to future success.

Einstein was devastated by the failure. Knowing that solar eclipses are rare and that the locations to view them are often not ideal, this was truly viewed as a setback. After getting himself back in order, Einstein went over his theory and realized that, had the expedition to photograph the solar eclipse been successful, his theory would have been proven wrong. Einstein revisited and adjusted his calculations.

It was not until 1915, a decade after initially publishing his work, that he updated the theory of special relativity with his general theory of relativity. Furthermore, he needed to wait an additional three years for another observable solar eclipse to provide supporting evidence. Two teams went out, including Campbell and Heber Curtis, to prove or disprove this new theory. This time the eclipse viewing was unhindered by Russian soldiers or clouds. While Curtis claimed that his photos supported Einstein's theory, Campbell's seemed to offer evidence to the contrary. However, Campbell's equipment was thought to have possibly been compromised, so he and his team held back on publishing their findings for fear that their reputation would be tarnished if they were later found to be wrong. The scientific community had to wait for yet another solar eclipse.

On May 29, 1919 an eclipse provided the evidence that would rocket Einstein to worldwide celebrity status. However, the cloud cover around that solar eclipse still left many in the scientific community unconvinced. It fell back to Campbell and his crew to either squash or justify the skepticism. On September 21, 1922, a solar eclipse was expected to be visible over Australia.

With better equipment, they went out amid much fanfare. Seven additional expeditions scattered around Australia set themselves up to observe and photograph the same solar eclipse. The resulting images proved Einstein's theory of general relativity, and the scientific community's understanding of light, matter, and energy has grown ever since.

All of this happened through a World War, a failed marriage for Einstein, several failed expeditions, as well as a lot of skepticism from the scientific community and beyond. Where would we be with our technology and understanding of the universe had clouds not blocked that first solar eclipse in 1914?

After learning all of this and how Campbell and his team continued to persist in their efforts to prove or disprove the theory, you may ask yourself, where are your own clouds? Can you imagine how pissed off you would be if you had taken tons of equipment on boats and donkeys, set up weeks ahead for this one moment, only to have a cloudy day ruin your trip? When I compare this to the internet going down for a few minutes or traffic getting a little tight, I understand that I really don't have any problems.

Lessons Learned: Failure is an Option

Failure is inevitable. Anticipate failure in all sizes and at all times, most of it unexpected and probably more than a little daunting. You cannot succeed without failure, so the more you fail, the more successful you will be. True failure comes from not getting started and not persisting.

The point in telling you this story is to illustrate just how important failure can be. Consider how many turning points worked in Einstein's favor. Consider also that if Campbell had been successful in Russia, it may have squelched inquiry into general relativity.

Another point is the shear strength of persistence. Campbell could have left after his first try, chalked it up to experience, and moved on doing his own thing. But he didn't. He kept pursuing his goal of proving or disproving Einstein's theories. Regardless of the outcomes of each expedition, he persisted.

> "There are two mistakes one can make along the road to truth: not going all the way, and not starting."
> -Buddha

Of course, failure can be a real pain in the ass. No one gets excited because they've failed. Have you ever lost $50,000 in your business due to an overlooked opportunity and were super happy about it? Probably not. But if, because of that loss, you put systems in place to make sure it didn't happen again and you landed over $200,000 in the next deal as a direct result, are you a happy camper? You bet you are. You're probably jumping-up-and-down-with-sticky-s'mores-fingers happy!

Learn from Mistakes

Keep in mind that the value of failure lies in learning from our mistakes. My kid and I were at a park one day when he was two years old. He was lifting himself between the seats of two picnic tables. He was doing these "kiddie dips" and having fun until he slipped and fell. He smacked his head on the concrete pad of the park shelter. He cried one of those super loud kid screams that make the world seem like it's crumbling in your very hands. After a minute of consoling him, I asked him if he wanted to try again. He jumped out of my arms and raced back over to those picnic tables. He hoisted himself up and started lifting himself up again. It was going to take more than a bit of concrete to stop him from getting better and learning from his failure. (And you can bet that he had a much better hold on those picnic table seats.)

Every once in a while, you or your business are going to hit a bit of concrete as you try to lift yourself up. When you fall, you accept the failure for what it is. A learning experience and nothing more.

Some of my family was there when my son hit the pavement. In a show of concern, my mom came over to the picnic tables and slapped and admonished them. "Mean picnic tables!" she said, making sure my son saw and heard her. But the picnic tables were not at fault. Neither was the concrete, nor the bird flying overhead. The blame, if there needs to be any, was on my son. He messed up because of a lack of experience or observation. That's it. Playing the victim will not prevent you from being victimized. It will only make victimization more frequent.

What you need to do with failure is realize what you can learn from it. In the case of my son, he could have decided never to try to balance on table seats again. He could decide to never stand again, never go to a park, never be with his grandma or his dad. But these reactions would be rooted in misplaced blame and would not have been in my son's best interest. From this simple example, you can see how mistakes and failures can guide you in any direction you choose. Will you focus on blame, or like my son, get back to solving this problem? Will you cower or will you conquer?

Conquer

The bold business owner will conquer. Cowering will only lead to a weakening of the spirit and character of your business. Think of the quickly evolving landscape of business right now. Amazon's CEO Jeff Bezos stated to his competitors, "Your margin is my opportunity." That should scare the hell out of anyone who has a business selling anything in retail, whether online or in brick-and-mortar. You can either blame Amazon for taking market share that may cut into your profits or you can thank them for being one of the movers who brought customers from buying with caution online to spending around $1.67 trillion in 2016 worldwide. That's trillion with a "t".

Either way, many failures (or challenges, if you prefer) are blessings in disguise. The pain is your privilege. You have the opportunity to expand your business, take on these challenges, and grow as failures attempt to mount against you.

Have you ever watched a professional fight? If so, you've seen the "tale of the tape" before the fight, which lists height, weight, and other stats pertaining to each fighter. What I find intriguing is that they include the professional fighter's history including the number of fights won and lost. It may read something like, "16 wins and 4 losses." Think about the fighter who has a history of 4 wins and 0 losses and compare him to a fighter who has 12 wins and 4 losses. One of the reasons this information is given is because people understand the value of experience, including the experience of losing.

> "Only in failure do you reach success. You can only get to the good stuff when you've done the hard stuff."
> -Kate Hudson

The Art of Failure

What are the feelings that can come from failure? Often the worst part about failure is not the actual event, but our reaction to it, our thoughts and feelings. We need to become aware of these feelings so that we can decide whether they are serving us in the best manner possible.

Regret

Regret is the biggest issue in failure.

"I should have done this."

"I could have done that."

"If only we had more time, resources, money, power or people."

If only we had more excuses! Regret is fine for a minute. After that, it's time to dust yourself off and realize the education you were just given. Your experience is a large part of your education.

Worry

Mary Schmich, in her book, *Wear Sunscreen: A Primer for Real Life*, defines the uselessness of worry by stating that "worrying is as effective as trying to solve an algebra equation by chewing bubblegum." This simple acknowledgement leads me to believe that worrying is essentially useless. Care and concern have their place in your life. Worrying about what could be or might be is only going to cause you to fret. Bold business owners do not fret. Bold business owners accept the challenges life throws at them. They catch them, take a bite as big as they see fit, and throw back the scraps.

> "**Worrying does not empty tomorrow of its troubles. It empties today of its strength.**"
> -Corrie Ten Moom

Disgrace

How bad would you feel if you lost your business and, in the process, happened to lose your retirement funds, your family's house, and your kid's college savings? You'd probably feel pretty devastated, right? Though it would be a terrible thing, it would not be without a silver lining. Essentially everything in life is education. Education is often expensive. What you need to do is avoid feeling or being disgraced. Acknowledge it and move on.

Mourning

This is one for the truly empathetic. In business, we are often asked, indirectly, to make a choice: undying compassion for the individual experiencing loss or realistic expectations for the betterment of the group. I recommend that you lean toward the good of the group. As the circus saying goes, the show must go on. Just because your grandma died does not mean that your employees and customers are not relying on you. Take the time to mourn, then get up. You have work to do. Make it clear to your employees during their interviews how your business treats issues like these. You don't need three weeks off for a funeral. That's just not healthy anyway. Live the life you were given to the fullest. The dead will appreciate you more if you do.

Procrastination

Procrastinate later. The stuff you put off is taking up space in your head for the stuff that you need to do now. It's best to just get it done or recognize that it's not worth doing at all. Touch everything on your desk only once. It should pass through your hands just one time. Just take care of it, resolve it, and leave that space in your head for the new and exciting things that will make you more money. Your mind has infinite space that can be quickly filled with infinite things that will limit you. Keep your mind's roadway clear for progress.

> "You proceed from a false assumption:
> I have no ego to bruise."
> -Leonard Nemoy

Assumptions of Convenience

Assumptions of convenience are essentially beliefs that allow for what you want to be true, though these beliefs can destine you for failure.

I was running late for work one day, and when I hustled outside to leave, I saw that my beloved Malibu had a flat tire. It was not flat enough that the wheel was on the ground, but it was noticeably squishy. My mind calculated what it would take to fill the tire with air. I could use a bike pump at home, which would take forever. I could drive to the local gas station, which would probably take longer. Alternatively, as my assumption of convenience came into play, I could make sure to drive 90 miles an hour down the highway to work, utilizing the power of centrifugal force to expand the tire to compensate for the lack of air. This option would not only allow me to get to work faster, it would also justify some questionably prudent speed. The decision was made and I was on my way. The centrifugal force is pretty sweet!

Driving on a flat tire is a bad idea. Driving on a flat tire at 90 miles per hour is an even worse idea. Luckily, I made it to work. However, that excursion cost me a tire, as the drive essentially overheated the tire and destroyed it from the inside out. That night of work, I earned $3.85 an hour for six hours, so about $23 before taxes. The replacement tire cost me over $80, plus installation. The assumption of convenience worked very well for immediate satisfaction. It worked against me in all other facets.

Lessons Learned: Assumptions of Convenience Are Everywhere

Make sure that when you make an assumption, it is founded on fact and not just hope.

All of these assumptions of convenience will make you, as a bold business owner, weaker. They will creep into your life and business disguised as opportunities. The thing about opportunity is that it doesn't always unveil itself as openly as we wish it would.

"The least questioned assumptions are often the most questionable."
-Stephen R. Covey

Are You a Frantic Business Owner?

I work with a lot of business owners. Every once in a while, I want to grab them by the shoulders and snap them out of whatever delusion they're in. Life doesn't have to be this hard, especially if you've started your own business and have it rolling. Did you start your business to get a heart attack at an awkwardly early age?

I give a little bit of slack to any owner who's been in

business less than two years or had a major loss in employees or customers. Occasionally, the universe wants to make sure you are as tough as you think you are. But if you're running around frantic, missing appointments, constantly running late, and are always moving at 120 mph all day every day, something is awry. Even race cars need to pit.

Let me be the first to admit that I set my internal cruise on 120 mph pretty often. People who know me would say that 120 mph is a casual speed for me. But let me follow that by saying I don't run that fast for 40 hours per week. I move that fast for maybe 30 hours a week, if not less. The beauty of running fast is finishing sooner; running fast and hard is almost a necessity for business owners. But, burning that much fuel with that much violence for more than 40 hours a week is crazy. You can just get a normal job and waste at least 20 hours a week and not be so stressed. The point is to run fast on the right track. Racing around for no reason is not progress; it's wasteful.

But that's not the story many business owners tell themselves. They are only ever thinking about how to get past the next deadline or presentation or meeting or sale or purchase or contract or commitment. They assume it will all be easier after that. Does that really ever happen? Does the end ever show up? We all delude ourselves with untruths that we are convinced are real every day.

Remember the last time you were late? Maybe it was traffic or time slipped away from you. As you were on your way to the appointment, you justified your tardiness in your head. It's only a couple minutes. They just chat in the beginning anyway. No one will notice. This isn't rude at all. They should be honored by my lateness.

I want to give credit to my wife here. Tardiness is a huge pet peeve of hers. I was the guy who tried to fit five hours of stuff in a one-hour time slot. Typically, I'd end up fitting it in an hour and 20 minutes, which I thought was pretty good. But it turns out that if you are routinely 20 minutes late to meeting your wife, she doesn't care why you were late. She (and most people) only care that you made them wait. The reason why you're late isn't important. The fact that you felt compelled to waste their time is the screaming detail that you need notice.

Respect those who are willing to make time for you. Even if you're paying them. Time is our most precious resource. Everyone has the same amount each day. Some people just value it more than others. I'm certain that whatever value people place on their time, they probably consider it more valuable than anyone else's. This includes yours, mine, and everyone else's time.

Here is my suggestion. Race when the race is ready and needed. Then go home and enjoy your life. You are too awesome to miss all of the fun you are having.

> "A sense of duty is useful in work but offensive in personal relations."
>
> -Bertrand Russell

My Dad...

I want to preface this short-ish story about my dad by making a few things clear. I respect my dad very much; if I had been in his place, with his experience, I would probably have done the same things. Second, as many others have said before, you are either a warning or an example. In many cases, my dad served as a warning for me. So for that, I thank you, Dad.

I come from a family of five kids, and I am right in the middle. My dad provided five kids with food and shelter for almost 30 years. That alone takes a toll on a guy. Add in a marriage that wasn't the best, and some inner emotional turmoil that may never get resolved without help. Just keep those emotions hidden where they belong, right?

During this funding of food and shelter for our family, my dad went through a few jobs, mostly in retail management. After getting the boot a few too many times due to circumstances outside of his control, he decided to go off on his own. (Sound familiar?) Now keep in mind that he was starting off on his own with no guaranteed income, no paid vacation, and very little in regard to a financial safety net. He also had seven mouths to feed and seven people to keep in a house with clothes and shoes. (Talk about risk!)

He ended up buying a milk delivery route which, when mentioned, seems to make people think he went to people's houses in his carriage and delivered the daily dose of milk in glass bottles. Though this story goes back in time, it doesn't go quite that far back. You see, this was a milk delivery business in the late '80s and through the '90s. He was delivering milk to grocery stores, schools, restaurants, and the like.

It turns out that milk is heavy and delivery trucks are expensive. Running a refrigerator that you can walk into gets expensive. Servicing towns that have fewer people living in them than the closest big box chain store has employees also leaves you with pretty low revenue numbers per stop. This led to one of the lessons I learned from my dad. Take care of the little guy, but take care of the big guys first. Without the big places buying milk in a substantial quantity, you cannot sustain taking care of only the smaller clients.

My dad delivered milk for almost 30 years, four to six days per week, and typically worked 10 to 14 hours per day. Hustling milk to these places and driving on to the next stop. Rinse and repeat. My dad's hope of a compelling future was limited in this business. So, his example provided a few lessons here as well.

One of the lessons was to have an endgame in mind. How will you leave your business? Do you want to sell your business and have it bring you some cash for your trouble? How can you make your business more valuable? The idea here, of course, is to sell your business at the highest possible price and have many people ready to buy it when you are ready to sell. But that's tough to do when what you're selling is a job with terrible hours, bad pay, and a very heavy product to move.

This brings us to another lesson. Have a business for which you can hire employees so you don't have to work so hard every day. When you have employees, you want to rely on them to help when the need arises. My dad eventually found one employee. The guy was super nice, and my dad tested his loyalty, though not intentionally.

At one point, my dad ended up with a serious bladder infection that landed him in the hospital. While laid up in a hospital, you can be certain your priorities change a bit. As a business owner, you find ways to survive. You also find ways to maintain the survival of your business, even from a hospital bed. Was this milk delivery business a legacy or was it how he was going to pay for some medical bills? Maybe both. My dad's employee helped save the business. He essentially ran two milk routes with a little help from my brother and brother-in-law.

The whole point of the lesson on gathering loyal employees is two-fold. Not everyone wants to work a ton in their life. Life is too short to spend it working more than you need to. Beyond that, every once in a while, stuff happens to you, your business, or your family that you never saw coming. Life will test you. Employees will help you pass that test. Employees will help you by picking up some (or all) of the slack in your absence or other employees' absence. Loyal, trustworthy, and smart employees are like gold to a business. Find a way to get them, train them, and keep them.

Lessons Learned: Breathe

The lesson to take here is to remember to breathe. In and out, slowly, and methodically as needed. I can breathe, currently, for free. When I do this, I can be in a meditative trance and calm my nerves if only for a few seconds. And I don't get cancer, so that's cool.

Keep Moving Forward

One powerful and positive thing I learned from my dad is to keep it moving. If you find that you did something that didn't work, try something else. Repeat that process until you succeed. The word "until" is key. Although success, as I desired, eluded my family during my childhood years, I can tell you that my dad continued to pursue success relentlessly, which makes me feel bad for those who achieve their dreams and become stagnant.

Lessons Learned: Appreciation

I often come across companies or people that I feel do not live up to my expectations. Either the results of their work are subpar or the customer service is lacking in both professionalism and an apparent desire for a customer. Presumably they are not intentionally doing a bad job. The recommendation is to appreciate that the people behind these companies have goals, desires, and knowledge, although they may not align with what you feel they should be doing. Appreciate that they are at least trying. Then find a better way to do it by going somewhere else or use this experience to create a new company.

Education is Everywhere

My dad taught me a ton about what to do and what not to do in my businesses. Some of these lessons I had to experience even after being exposed to them in order to really solidify the knowledge.

Use your experiences as you go about your day getting an education. Watching the systems of fast food restaurants, listening to how other companies answer their phones, even discovering how huge hotels stay clean with their array of employees.

All of these experiences can broaden your knowledge. All you need to do is become aware of this vast education. Then actually implement what you learn.

Lessons I learned from my dad include:

1) Avoid trading money for time. You will always give away more time than you mean to and you have a limit to how much time you actually have to trade.

2) Family time is important. Many members of my family resented my dad while he was working so many hours. It was a vicious cycle. We resented him so he kept working. He kept working so we resented him.

3) Some people just need to work with their hands to earn a living. I have a tough time justifying not working with my hands for a living. There is a pride that comes with working with your hands. But like most areas of pride, it can cost you. Pride is expensive.

4) Know how to fix things if you need to. If a zombie apocalypse comes, do you think the survivors will celebrate having an author or a guy that moves thousands of pounds of milk a day?

Work that is subject to weather can be tough. Snowy days or sunny days, people will eat cookies and cereal. Which means they will consume milk. Driving through bad weather is not fun and makes for a long day with no added profit for your troubles.

Celebrate great vendors. The people that delivered the product to my dad came in two types, awesome and probably drunk. The awesome people were rewarded and helped in any way my dad could. The probably drunk people drove their trucks into anything and everything. My dad did everything possible to get more awesome people for the safety, liability as well as knowing that the alternative was filled with problems that needed quick solutions.

5) Love who you work for. My dad befriended just about

every one of his clients. To my disillusionment at the time, he chatted with almost every customer during every stop. A quick conversation went well towards keeping the relationship moving. He always brought a smile to his clients.

6) Solve your problems. Whether it was a broken down truck or a missed delivery, my dad did not go to a Board of Directors to try to discover a solution. He just took action to solve the problem. Immediately and diligently until it was solved.

7) Get your kids to work for cheap. Wait a second...

Battle Tested
by Kate Lind, Aspect Compliance
aspectcompliance.com

I began my campaign finance compliance business in 2009 to fill a need in political committees. Through industry experience, I had gained a deep understanding of this need and believed that I had a solution. Initially, I began providing these services to a single client. After just a few months, the workload for this client suddenly exploded to a point beyond which I could no longer manage the work without staff, office space, and improved processes.

After a couple of missteps, I eventually had the fortune to find myself with a team of loyal, hardworking staff who lent their blood, sweat, and tears to the effort alongside me. When deadlines loomed, members of my staff would show up to work in the morning with overnight bags and pillows, knowing that they would be at the office well into the wee hours of the morning. It was trial by fire, and 24 months after my business opened its doors, we were exhausted but battle-tested and still standing. It took several more years for the business to evolve to a place where the pit in my stomach—fear that we had missed something, that a mistake had been made, that the business would fail—finally got some relief.

New business owners may need to be prepared to go years without a day off, let alone a vacation. If you are bootstrapping your new business as I did, you may have the added need to earn an additional stream of income. I was able to transition from my existing full-time job into a part-time role while building the business and representing the occasional legal client on the side.

The biggest struggle I ran into was settling on a pricing model that was palatable and affordable to our clients, while generating a profit (or in the early years, at least breaking even). Our services were new to many of our clients, and we were underpricing them in an effort to establish a client base and gain experience. Eventually, we were able to establish a pricing structure that was both fair and workable. We have devoted a great deal of effort to making our processes more efficient so that we can charge less than our competition while remaining profitable. It is important to me to continue offering our services for an affordable price, while ensuring that our employees earn decent pay and benefits and are able to enjoy a healthy work-life balance. While we still experience the occasional long days and weekend hours, they are few and far between and (to my knowledge) no one sleeps at the office anymore.

Barriers to building a successful business vary by industry, but I have to think that a few guiding principles should apply across the board. It is my experience that starting a new business requires hard work, an understanding that there will be tough times, and an expectation that you and your business will struggle through some pretty lean months or even years. For me, it helped that I was financially unable to consider failure to be an option, and that I was blissfully ignorant of what I didn't know. Not every day will be a good one, and you will make some very real sacrifices for your business. If you don't love what you're doing, I have a hard time imagining an outcome of professional and personal success for you. Fortunately, for me, the rewards of being a successful business owner have justified the risks and the struggles.

Chapter 4

So, what do you do?

66

"I'm tough, ambitious and I know exactly what
I want. If that makes me a bitch, Okay."

99
                                                    -Madonna

This book is as much for me as it is for you. This book is my "what." It's the thing that I've been training for. It's what I can offer to help others succeed so they can do their part in making the world a better place. In the end, bold business owners help others much more than they help themselves.

Your what in this chapter is both what your basic business will be as well as what you need to do in order to make it successful. In this chapter, we will work to help you find what you want in your business and what business will help you attain this. Your business should work for you more than you work for it. This should be by design.

A common pitfall of a new business owner is to start a business based on a hobby or something they are good at or enjoy doing.

Often, this leads to a failed business due to the lack of a solid market, conflicting desire for growth, or limited potential. For example, you may love biking. Opening a retail bike store may be a dream. However, the retail hours, internet competition, and general crowd of bikers that may sustain a bike store may or may not be available where you open it. This can lead to some vivid dreams being crushed awfully quickly (not to mention expensively).

> "*You cannot escape the responsibility of tomorrow by evading it today.*"
>
> -Abraham Lincoln

Suppose you already have a business and you have come to realize that it may not survive the challenging transition from dream to reality. What then? You have a few options. You can suffer through until something breaks (you, the business, or your bank account); you can innovate, take risks and do everything you can to grow your business; or you can close up shop and try something new. The first solution is weak. The latter two solutions are bold.

This guide is meant to help you create a business that will give you the enjoyment and success you desire. Only a rare business owner includes constant struggle as a part of their business plan. But believe me, struggles and challenges in your business will show up without encouragement.

> "*Since everything is a reflection of our minds, everything can be changed by our minds.*"
>
> -Buddha

Oops

I'd like to tell you another story, a story about what brought this book into your hands. Remember that 1979 Chevy Malibu station wagon? I bought that car when I was 17 years old. Even as a middle child, you need to create new paths. My parents had a rule for my two older siblings: you can't have a car until you are 18. I understand why they had this rule; I get a little queasy just thinking about having a driving teenager. But, back then, I challenged the practicality of it. I was 16 and decidedly bold (not to mention that the idea of not being able to drive a girl on a date seemed less than appealing).

I had a job at a local movie theater. It was a nice place to work, but it was on the opposite end of town, so my mom had to drive me to and from work. This got a little old for her since my shifts often ended at 10 p.m. or later. So after a few months of being chauffeured to and from work, I convinced my parents that allowing me to own a car was only logical. When they conceded, I ponied up the cash and bought my first car. And it broke down. A lot. I think I pushed that car more than I drove it.

That is experience you do not forget.

Alas, making $3.85 an hour at a movie theater does not make you rich. It basically pays for a little food, a bit of gas, and an enormous amount of insurance premiums. It turned out I was working to pay for the car that allowed me to get to work. So when the car did break down, I relied on my own two hands and a few friends to help me fix it as cheaply as possible. This meant I had to learn the ins and outs of how cars work pretty quickly. I became an expert at "noise diagnostics." I already had a pretty strong mechanical aptitude; this just let me put it to use.

Thanks to my newfound expertise in auto mechanics, I got a job at a local auto-parts store, which gave me discounts on parts I always seemed to need. That led to a job at a repair shop, where I used my newly acquired skills to wrench on other people's cars. While I was getting my hands dirty, I was going to college studying graphic design.

Combining the auto repair and graphic design led to a job fixing printers, which led to starting my own printer repair business, which led me to establishing a virtual receptionist company. This, in turn, led to a business-coaching practice. And that business-coaching practice led to writing this book.

Would I have ever been able to guess that buying an unreliable car at the age of 17 would lead me through the maze that ended with this book in your hands? Nope.

What decisions in your life have led to you being where you are now? What decisions challenged your success? Trace backward to identify the decisions you made and the actions you took that led to starting your own business:

1. _____

2. _____

3. _____

4. _____

> "Most of my major disappointments have turned out to be blessings in disguise. So whenever anything bad does happen to me, I kind of sit back and feel, well, if I give this enough time, it'll turn out that this was good, so I shouldn't worry about it too much"
>
> -William Gaines

It's weird to look back and see what led to where we are now. Was it all coincidence, or were we guided? How would you prefer to answer that question? If you knew you were in control over where you'll go in the future, where would you choose to go? What would you like to accomplish?

I've been told by countless small business owners that they started their businesses in an effort to take control of their own destiny. How powerful is that? Every decision they make and every person they meet steers them toward the goal of controlling this destiny.

Lessons Learned: There is No Such Thing as a Coincidence

Things that appear to be coincidences can be explained by either or both of these two theories, depending on your beliefs:

1) The universe is watching and guiding you toward exactly what you seek.

2) Your mind, both the conscious and subconscious, is aware of what you want and helps you take action to achieve those goals.

With this in mind, I want to warn you of a possible pitfall. Think about the idea of "controlling your own destiny." It has an almost poetic ring to it, doesn't it? It sets you up as the hero, entering the story to kick some major ass. Fire up the symphony—we are about to go on an epic journey of brutal battles that you'll rise above and conquer.

But wait, wait, wait.

What destiny? "Destiny," by itself, doesn't describe what you are really after. How would you define the destiny you are chasing? I doubt that anyone would claim, "My destiny is to work 80 hours a week fumbling through paperwork, catching up on client calls, and losing my train of thought 52 times a day." For many small business owners, this seems to be the destiny they arrive at.

Do you know why?

They never defined which destiny they wanted. Destiny comes from the same root word as destination, the Latin word destinare, which means "to make firm." What is your ultimate destination? Success, as we will soon learn, is not to be considered a destination alone. Success is also a part of the journey itself. However, you need an endpoint; you need a destination to move toward. Otherwise, you'll only be successful at being aimless and lost.

Confused yet? Read on. Luckily, realizing that you are confused is the first step to gaining clarity.

Lessons Learned: Become Aware of Your Experience as Education

Figuring out your "what" is actually a lot of fun. It can also be a lot of work. For example, I know I don't want to have a business that has set hours, such as a retail store. I know this because I worked many years stuck to a rigid hourly schedule. I could have just read this book and saved a TON of wasted time. Now I know one of my "whats" is to be able to work when and where I want.

The King Who had Two Kingdoms

There once was a king with two kingdoms. The kingdoms were beautiful and flourishing and brought great joy to the king and his subjects. The problem was that the king was tired of having two kingdoms. He considered getting more kingdoms, but two kingdoms were already a lot of work. He wanted to grow his kingdom in some other way. He wanted more, yet he could not define exactly what more was.

The king heard of a poor shaman who was travelling through his kingdom with nothing but a blanket, a loincloth, and a magic lamp. The lamp was said to bring you double what you asked it for. The shaman was preaching to many of the peasants, guiding them to find happiness in their lives.

The king shouted to his soldiers to gather the shaman so he could learn from the shaman and find out more about the lamp he carried.

The soldiers brought the shaman to the king. The king welcomed the shaman to his castle and introduced himself. The shaman bowed to the king and thanked him for his gracious hospitality.

The king remarked, "Surely I can help you make your way through my kingdoms, shaman. How do you make it on your own with only your few possessions?"

"My dear King, I am but a poor man spreading knowledge to some passersby. I do not need much to make my journey," the shaman answered quietly.

"What is it that you take with you? I see a blanket, a loincloth, and a shiny lamp. Tell me about the lamp."

"It is an heirloom from my family from many generations ago. It is my only true possession."

"Is it true that the lamp will grant you double what you ask of it?"

"Yes, Your Highness, that is true. Though I would never ask it for anything."

The king ordered the guards to grab the lamp from the shaman and throw him out of the castle. The king was given the lamp and ran to his chambers. "Surely I will get what I am looking for with this magic lamp!" the king shouted to himself. He rubbed the lamp and asked the lamp for 100 gold pieces.

The lamp replied, "100 gold pieces? Why not ask for 200 gold pieces?"

The king was ecstatic. "You are correct, lamp! Give me 200 gold pieces!"

"Silly King, why ask for 200 when you could have 400 gold pieces?" the lamp replied slyly.

The king was amazed. "What a great idea! Give me 1000 gold pieces!"

"1000 gold pieces seems too low for a king such as you. Why don't you ask for 2000 gold pieces?" the lamp replied.

The king stood up and demanded, "Lamp, give me 10,000 gold pieces!"

The lamp replied, "Only 10,000 gold pieces? Wouldn't you be happier with 20,000 gold pieces?"

You can imagine the king's amazement. This continued until the king exhausted himself and died alone in his room with the lamp in his hand.

Lessons Learned: Be Careful What You Desire

Wants are a fickle thing. You may want something, but once you have it, you may decide you want to get rid of it, like a brownie that becomes part of your thighs. Your short-term wants must align with your long-term desires.

There are many lessons in this story, the first of which is to have a destination in mind and stick with it until it is achieved, or at least almost achieved. Once you find yourself approaching the destination, it's OK to challenge yourself further. Continuing to push beyond unreached milestones will be futile.

A lesson on decision-making could also be extracted here. The king could have easily decided that 1000 gold pieces was pretty sweet and moved on with his life. The mind of an entrepreneur is rarely so focused, though it often needs to be.

Another lesson to learn from the king—focus. Or treating people right. Or respecting power that you do not understand. Or making sure your actions lead to the actual tangible results you are after.

> *"You are the master of your own environment. You've got your own head, your own mind. So once you figure out what you want for yourself, you have to create the proper environment to make sure you can live all the things you want."*
> -Tyrese Gibson

We want to be careful to avoid the trap that was alluded to in the king's tale. You want to achieve your notion of success, but we know that success is a journey.

Working Hard to Make it Grow
by Scott Robison, Integration Bodywork LLC
integrationbodywork.net

As recently as 5 years ago, I was telling myself that I wasn't interested in the risk of being self-employed. Yet, here I am, a small business owner working hard to make it grow.

A little context: I have a BS in Physics, and after a short stint as a mediocre PhD student, I tried my hand at teaching high school and personal training. Neither was a good fit. Then I found massage and bodywork, and I knew I had found the right path.

Massage therapy is pretty flexible when it comes to employment. You can be an employee, an independent contractor, or self-employed. I started as an independent contractor so I could practice my craft on my own terms and let someone else run the business, but I finally went out on my own.

Here's the thing about opening an independent massage practice: You need almost no infrastructure to support it. You could probably operate a successful practice with nothing more than a spare bedroom, a massage table, a phone, and a datebook. There's almost no need for a formal business plan. Is there an Elements Massage or Massage Envy franchise in your town? Then you know right away that there is plenty of demand for your services, no market research required.

The areas in which I've had to work hardest to learn have been marketing, sales, and systems design. I'm combining marketing and sales into one skill. For me, that's the process of finding potential clients and convincing them to book. I've had to work hard to learn how to talk about what I do in a way that is not only accurate, but also convinces people that they need my services. Lots of practice, working with a business coach, and reading books like Book Yourself Solid have been a big help.

The second skill I've had to learn, and definitely the most difficult to master, is systems design. Having a systematic method for every part of the business frees up my brain and creativity for more important things. It also ensures that things don't get missed by accident. I'm a one-man shop, there's no redundancy. Having systems in place definitely makes my life easier. The E-Myth Revisited and The Four-Hour Work Week have been great resources and inspiration in this regard.

Systems also provide the potential for scalability. My goal is to have at least one other therapist employed as an independent contractor in a year and to sell the business in three years. Systems ensure that everyone's clients will have the same great experience and that everyone gets paid accurately, whether I'm there or not.

The best method I've found for developing business systems is to start with a best guess, and then iterate. Keep the things that work well, drop the things that don't, or maybe try them in a different order. Build lists, build spreadsheet macros, and most importantly, write down the steps in order. Once the system is optimized, you probably won't need to refer to the written document anymore, but it's a good reference. You can also use it to train future employees or the people you sell to.

I've only been in business for about 6 months, and only full-time for 4 months. Honestly, I still have no idea what I'm doing, but with some hard work and thoughtful practice, I'm getting better everyday.

Once you have defined your what, you can move on to find your ideal business. What do you love to do? What can you imagine yourself doing for the next decade or two?

Finding the right business can be tough. You will come up with an idea for a business and hang out in a honeymoon phase before you even have your business plan started. You will essentially have a crush on your non-existent business. Lights will be brighter, days will be longer, you'll have a skip in your step and a serenade in your heart.

Then you actually need to take action, create your business, and get it moving. Once it's off the ground, you need to improve it. Keep the passion alive, because this is going to be a long relationship. And speaking of improvement, who is really more successful, the person who achieves and plateaus or the person who continually strives for improvement?

> *"We have a strategic plan.*
> *It's called doing things."*
> -Herb Kelleher

What are You Going to Sell, and Who is Going to Buy?

Now you need to figure out what you are going to sell and to whom you are going to sell it. In theory, you can create a company and have a website rolling and available all day, every day, selling whatever you can get your hands on. Or you can open a retail store. Or a restaurant. The choice is yours. Here's a simple questionnaire to get your gears turning:

1. What is your ideal business?
2. Describe a business person you admire. What do they do?
3. Three years from now, where do you want to be? Where do you want your business to be?
4. What will success look like?
5. Describe your typical Tuesday afternoon six months

from now.

6. Describe your typical Saturday evening six months from now.
7. How many hours worked per week is too many?
8. Do you want to work directly with every customer?
9. Do you want to expand beyond just yourself?
10. How do you plan to exit the company? Sell it, close it, drop it like it's hot when you die?
11. Does your family come into your decision-making process?
12. How much money do you want to make?
13. How much work are you willing to do?

Lessons Learned: Reading Alone Won't Save You Money

Hold on while I go get my soapbox... If I were reading this book on a bus or in an office or on an airplane, I may have a hard time answering all these questions at just this moment. But remember to come back to this list before you get your business rolling. Get some answers or at least be aware of the questions. Reading them alone will not suffice. That's like getting a check and not cashing it.

These are all pretty simple questions on the surface, but the answers have loads of feelings and thought behind them. Take the time to consider them. I suggest you mark this page. Every time you have a few minutes to spare, look at the list and choose a question to consider.

For example, how many business owners do you know who started a business because they were good at a particular skill? They grew the business to a plateau and either decided to get out, grow their business to include employees, or live a life of self-employment, which is essentially owning their job. Do you want to be that person? Take a few minutes now to potentially save yourself thousands of dollars and countless hours later.

Don't get me wrong. I was that person and in some ventures I still am. I started a printer repair company because I was a damn good printer repair technician. I just happened to have zero business skills. I didn't know what I didn't know. Allow me to save you some time.

Your business selection does not have to be perfect. Do you know why serial entrepreneurs exist? I used to think that serial entrepreneurs weren't committed. How can you keep starting businesses instead of continually growing the one you have? The answer is pretty simple. Starting businesses can give you a high not seen since your first crush, and selling a business is almost as exhilarating, at least when you get paid.

> *"Being an entrepreneur isn't really about starting a business. It's a way of looking at the world: seeing opportunity where others see obstacles, taking risks where others take refuge."*
>
> -Michael Bloomberg

Sometimes you need to make big decisions and take big risks. At some point, I simply knew I would start my own business. I decided it was going to happen. The problem was that I didn't know what business I was going to start. I sat down with a pen and a piece of a paper and had brainstorming session. I wrote down everything that I could think of that I might enjoy or could learn to enjoy.

Lessons Learned: Brainstorming

I cannot recommend brainstorming enough. I have an 8-foot whiteboard in my office, and I recommend you get the biggest whiteboard you can find and hang it on the biggest wall you have. This will remove the limitations of boundaries when you brainstorm.

The next step is to write, write, and write some more. Do not judge, criticize, or belittle anything you write for more than a few seconds. Do not remove an item just because you don't feel it'll work. Your thoughts come to you for a reason, and maybe that reason was to trigger another thought. Get it all written down and let the conversation flow.

So write, write, and write some more. When the dust settles, then you can go about your serious judging.

I went to school for graphic arts, so that was on the list. I love funny t-shirts, so I jotted that down. I added in a bunch of hobbies and things that seemed interesting. But, to be completely honest, I went about my process of discovery completely backwards. I was choosing "what business" before "what will I be doing in my business."

The difference is basic, though important. What business is basically the product or service will you be selling. Will you be a baker hocking donuts or a CNC manufacturer selling custom fabricated metal creations? The what will I be doing in my business details the ins and outs necessary to create it. For example, if you want to open a bakery, you'll probably need to wake up at 3 a.m. or so to start making donuts and bread. I am guessing you'll also gain 100 pounds over a very short period of time. The what business is the bakery, the what will you be doing is waking up really early and making donuts. Imagine starting a bakery and not getting up until 8 a.m. Your target clients have come and gone before your dough has even had time to rise. Though you may love the idea of owning a bakery, if baking at 3 a.m. isn't for you, neither is a running a bakery.

Check out more:
www.drawincustomers.com

> *"Whether you can do or dream you can, begin it. Boldness has genius, magic and power in it. Begin now."*
> -W.H. Murray

After all of the writing and brainstorming ideas came out, I looked at my lists and doodles and decided on some criteria for judging them. First, I crossed off the ideas I thought had no chance of success. Then I went through and rated each idea between one and ten on three criteria: fun, time, and feasibility. That led me to printer repair.

Clearly my idea of fun was a little odd. But I loved talking with people and I loved not being stuck in an office. I also enjoyed making money while driving. In my world, fixing things is just about the most fun a person can have.

You see, I was already a printer repair technician. I was great at it. But I knew I could only go so far working for someone else; there was one more step to take, and I decided to take it.

Not unlike the employees of any small business, I had been making about $14 an hour fixing printers, with no benefits and limited vacation. I hated the office where I worked, because it was a poorly lit warehouse, and one of my co-workers blared annoying sports radio day in and day out. I felt I was becoming dumber; the job I was in had zero potential for growth, and I was bursting with the desire to grow.

So I was a great printer-repair technician with a job I disliked in an environment that was torturous, earning mediocre money with no possibility of growth. The decision to leave in order to start my own gig was not exactly hard. I could get a job making peanuts anywhere. This is one of those grass is greener times when the grass you are on is just a pile of weed-filled mud.

The risk I was taking was negligible.

I committed to myself to starting my own business. I didn't know much about business. I also had no idea that I didn't know much about business. I knew I needed a website and business cards. So I learned what I needed to learn to get a website going and created a site from scratch coding all of the HTML, if you remember those days. I had some business cards made. Then I figured I should probably go out and sell.

🎓 Lessons Learned: Learning

In life and business, you'll need to learn things you didn't anticipate. I had to learn HTML and website coding. My receptionists at Calls On Call learn things about construction and massage from their clients. You know that you'll need to learn some things, like taxes and accounting. Other things, like web design, are completely unexpected.

There are many things you may need to learn to save money and time and to make your life, as a whole, more well-rounded. There is no such thing as being too knowledgeable.

Wait...What?

Let's talk about you and your business. If you're trying to figure out which business to start, let's begin with some key questions.

What kind of hours do you want to work? Don't tell me something crazy like 90 hours a week or something. That's not a pace you can maintain long term. (And why would you want to?)

_____

What's the location of where YOU do the work? Is it a kitchen, an office, or on the road? Remember, it can be literally anywhere. Where do you want to work?

_____

_____

What kind of money do you want to make? Will you be happy with the potential earnings the business you are considering starting can provide you?

_____

Who has to approve of your business? This may include your spouse, family, friends, colleagues, church, etc. Most of us have roots of some kind. Take them into account here.

_____

_____

How much business would you need to get to keep your business running successfully? Are you willing to sell for your business?

_____

_____

What sort of capital will you need to start your business? How much do you have now? How much can you get, and where will you get it? (Don't let this question scare you—you can always find a way. You just have to find it.)

_____

What room for growth are you planning for? For example, you may consider franchising your business, adding employees, adding services or products, etc.

_____

_____

_____

So, what do you do?

Who will buy your products or services? Are you OK dealing with them as often as they purchase? (Some customer demographic groups can be more annoying than others.)

_____

_____

Who will work with you? Will you have employees? Will you have subcontractors?

_____

_____

What do you need to learn in order to start your business?

_____

_____

What timeline do you have for starting your business?

_____

Now, brainstorm some business options that fit these answers as closely as possible.

_____

_____

_____

_____

_____

_____

When you go back through your brainstorm list, whittle it down based on your gut and your experience. Importantly, consider the fun, time, and feasibility criteria that I mentioned earlier.

> *"Dream big, work hard, and don't be an asshole."*
>
> -Mike Shinoda

Innovation is the Key

One more tiny detail. When you decide what business you are going to start and run, don't fall in love with it. One of the most challenging and necessary things in business is innovation. If you're not in the technical world and don't own a business like the old Bell Labs or Google that demand innovation, you can easily get lost in the day-to-day shuffle of your business. Every business needs to innovate, whether they are considered technical or not. Sam Walton brought the check-out aisles to the front of the store after seeing it done in a few smaller places. Even carpet cleaners keep coming out with the next best thing to get the job done.

> *"Innovation is an option here. If things are not failing, you are not innovating enough."*
>
> -Elon Musk

Between 1991 and 1993, IBM lost over 30% of its value due to declining hardware revenue. It took a big drop for IBM to take notice and attempt to innovate to recover. Businesses often slowly drop in certain areas as the need for their product or service dwindles. In this case the drop was happening quite quickly. Remember Webcrawler and other web search engines at the frontier of search functionality for the internet? They started out quite innovative and dropped by the wayside as they were outdone by their competitors.

So, what do you do?

Companies must innovate to survive as well as thrive, and you, as the leader of your company, must decide when and how you will innovate. Change typically means pain, so many businesses avoid it. That's a sure recipe for eventual failure.

An advantage of implementing new and exciting things is that the company culture doesn't get stale. Every employee and business owner has gone through the mild depression of feeling like it's Groundhog Day. When you introduce new ideas and work on implementing them, you bring new life to your business. Not every new idea will be successful. Most will not. But how many innovative ideas do you really need to be successful?

Fedex tried Zapmail in 1984 to compete with fax machines. They lost almost $350 million in just over two years. Steve Jobs fumbled after he was booted from Apple with NeXT, a computer workstation for educators. He lost hundreds of millions of investor dollars. You know that Dyson vacuum company? Sir James Dyson went through over 5,000 failed prototypes and all of his savings over 15 years.

Bold business leaders innovate, adapt, and grow through adversity and challenges that are inherent in business. Show me a business owner with no implementation challenges, and I will show you a business owner with no business.

> *"Business is about people. It's about bold ideas, bold small ideas or bold large ideas."*
>
> -Tom Peters

Now go start your **BOLD** Business.

**Share your stories:
coach@drawincustomers.com**

A Daunting Experience
by Tina Hallis, Ph.D, The Positive Edge
thepositiveedge.org

Being a new entrepreneur can be a daunting experience! You suddenly have to be responsible for every part of the business—sales, marketing, products/services, finance, etc. Setting priorities and staying focused is a major challenge I constantly face. I'm easily distracted and can find an abundance of interesting information and "experiments" to try to drive my business.

I've found the insights and tips in two books to be incredibly helpful: The One Thing - The Surprising Simple Truth Behind Extraordinary Results by Gary Keller & Jay Papasan and Essentialism: The Disciplined Pursuit of Less by Greg McKeown. The titles really say it all. What is the one essential thing you should be doing right now? This takes some reflection, analysis, and self-discipline. Check them out if you share my need for focus. I'm still working on consistently applying what I've learned from both of them.

Another thing I've found on my entrepreneurial journey is that many people are happy to give you advice and to tell you what you SHOULD be doing. It can be confusing and overwhelming. I can't do everything and I really want to use my strengths and stay true to my values. This ties back to the challenge of focusing. I have to keep reminding myself that there are many paths to creating a successful business and I have to find my own way and focus on that. This doesn't mean I can't learn from others or try different things, but in the end, I can't copy the journey of others exactly; I have to find what works for me. I'm fortunate to have met entrepreneurs who have taken a variety of approaches to their business, so I know there really are multiple ways to be successful. I encourage you to consider your own strengths and values when choosing your business strategies.

I love sharing the story of how The Positive Edge came to be, because it shows that I've not only learned the theory behind increasing our positivity for resilience and motivation, but that I've had first-hand experience discovering how important and helpful it can be.

My background is in biotechnology. It was 2011 when I was at a continuing education class and fortuitously discovered positive psychology. Here was a science that focused on helping people live a better life! I was so excited to share this newfound knowledge with my colleagues at work. So I put together a talk to share it with them even though I was a scientist at the time. It was great fun, and I was so sad when it was over. Then someone mentioned that I could probably give this talk at a local library.

I'll never forget. It was Wednesday, November 7. When I came to work, I noticed the first thing on my calendar was a meeting with my boss. This was kind of unusual because he was normally offsite, in another state. I went downstairs to the conference room where we were to meet and opened the door. There sat my boss, and there sat HR (Human Resources). I knew what this meant. Many of my friends and coworkers had been laid off in the past few years. It was my turn. Packing up my stuff from 11 years of work was an out-of-body experience. Things can change so fast in our lives. I took this change as a sign that I was supposed to spread my newfound positive psychology information beyond the walls of my current company. How interesting that it happened on the day I planned to give my first positivity talk!

A week later I was talking to my dad on the phone, and he asked a very innocent question. He said, "How is the job search going?" I told him I wasn't looking for another job. Then I swallowed, paused, and said that I had decided to start my own company. I could feel the blood drain from my face and the knots in my stomach tightening. That was the first time I had said it out loud. It was a major decision, not only because I was totally reinventing myself, but because I had been the main breadwinner with all of the benefits for our family. The future was a big scary unknown. I think it was three months before the waves of nausea finally subsided.

I was passionate and determined that I needed to share what I had learned in order to help more people. And I knew that if there was one place we needed help staying positive, it was at work. So my new mission was to get into organizations to teach people how to shift their thinking, help them realize that they had a choice, so they could get better at seeing the positive and have more enjoyable work experiences and better lives.

During this time of transition, I was incredibly fortunate that I had already spent a year learning the insights and practices from positive psychology. I don't know how people get through such stress and uncertainty without this type of information. I know it made a big difference for me, and it's been an important part of my personal development and growth. Now I'm honored to share what I've learned to help others navigate the changes and uncertainties in their work.

Chapter 5

" *"You can't connect dots looking forward; you can only connect dots looking backwards. So you have to trust that the dots will somehow connect in your future. You have to trust in something—your gut, destiny, life, karma, whatever. This approach has never let me down, and it has made all the difference in my life."* **"**

-Steve Jobs

The answer to the question of when to start a business is similar to that of when to get married, to have a kid, or to retire. It's rarely the perfect time to start a business. Even if the perfect time should arise, you may still find yourself too apprehensive to actually start your business.

So when is the ideal time to start a business? The answer is now. As in right now. Today. This moment. If you are considering starting a business, commit to doing one thing to move in that direction. File a Limited Liability Company (LLC), get a domain name, start drawing a logo, come up with a name, or quit your job. Do something. Commit yourself to working to be as successful as you want to be.

Will your business flop? Maybe. But who cares? What if it's a success? What if you had started your business two weeks ago?

> **"Don't worry about failure. You only have to be right once."**
>
> -Drew Houston

Where Will You be in Two Weeks?

The world is full of slackers and people who live in fear of exploring outside their world. They're afraid to ask a very important question: What if...? Are you OK with being a slacker who fears failure? Can you ride a bike? Have you ever fallen off a bike? If you fell off a bike tomorrow, and two weeks from now I asked you if you could ride a bike, would you tell me no?

Get on your bike.

> **"If you really want to do something you will find a way. If you don't, you will find an excuse."**
>
> -Jim Rohn

No Excuses

You've probably recognized that I can be a bit abrasive, especially when I hear silly excuses. Often people refer to me as pompous or, if they're kind, as brutally honest.

I am OK with that. Don't get me wrong, I'm not here to make people hate me. In fact, it's in my best interest to have everyone like me. (Or at least people who read books like this.) Every once in awhile though, someone needs to be kicked in the behind to get moving.

Let me give you an example.

I had a meeting with a potential client to go over Calls On Call so I could explain how we could get his company's phone answered. After a few meetings and a lot of dragged out maybes and "We're growing so we have our elbows pretty deep in something else…" excuses, I was getting frustrated. I hear the same excuses from other prospects, just like anyone in sales. Sales is a game of buyers being liars and sales people trying to crack the buyer's code to lying.

So, I met with the guy one last time at his office, and I learned three things: He is always late for meetings, he has a part-time office manager who is struggling to deal with her boss, and his only technician is his son, a lazy, dopey-looking kid. While this business owner clearly needed my help, answering his phones wouldn't be the half of it.

As we started talking about phones, he blocked my pitch by explaining that they had uber-sophisticated software that's hard to learn and harder to understand. (Keep in mind this is for appliance repair—the fields that need to be filled out include name, address, phone number, whatever appliance is broken, and what the problem is. After that, you can set a time for a technician to go to the customer's place and fix away. End of complication.)

Appliance Repair Guy droned on and on about his business. While I could see there was a fit and some potential, he was not interested in resolving his issues. He just wanted to talk about them and have sales people like me listen intently and assure him that he was doing great, that things would get better.

At the end of the meeting, I was frustrated. Not from the "no" I received, but from the time wasted while he described the no. In fact, he never actually said no out loud. I couldn't get a no out of this guy even if I tried. I stood up and told him it was great meeting and reiterated that he had a growing business, which was our forte. I told him that if he was interested, he should call me because "I don't chase prospects."

I received an email from him later in which he stated how

he resented the fact that I had said I "don't chase" prospects. This struck me as odd. I didn't mean for it to be offensive. I meant that I had to spend my time on prospects who were likely to sign up with us. Spending time on a bunch of meetings with one person was not a valuable use of my time. Or his.

Lessons Learned: The Meaning of Communication

The rule is that communication is defined not by what is said but by the meaning that is received. So I clearly failed in this example. As an excellent BOLD business owner, you'll be best served if you can listen to others and consider what they say without forgetting to think about what you say and how they may interpret it.

A few months later, I ran across his business on the Web. So I called him up, and lo and behold, he committed! He was ready to sign up in July and make a move to grow his business by actually taking action. July was several weeks away. In hindsight, the fact that he wouldn't sign a contract right away was probably a red flag, but I appreciate that people are busy.

I mentioned the July start date to my receptionists, and they stopped me in my tracks. Vacations were happening, new clients were starting, and July was not a good idea. But August was a great idea. So I told Appliance Repair Guy that July can't happen, but August is the ticket. Great, he said, he'd call me in August.

I followed up with him in August a few times. No one answered the phone. September—again, a bunch of voicemails. I emailed, but got no reply. This guy was ready to trust us as his first line of communication with potential customers, something we don't take lightly, but now, he was hiding from us. This is why I avoid chasing.

So goes the plight of the sales person. That's why sales people who do well get paid so much. They have to tolerate a lot of abuse to get to those sales.

> *"In real life, strategy is actually very straightforward. You pick a general direction and implement like hell."*
> -Jack Welch from Winning

While avoiding some other task, I was cleaning off my desk and going through some notes when I came across the appliance repair guy's name again. It had been more than six months since our last encounter. I don't believe in coincidences, so I picked up the phone. I figured that since this guy was ready to do business with us six months earlier, maybe he was ready to go now. (How long does it take to get a business in order?)

He had an auto-responder setup. You know the kind. The pinnacle of customer service with an automated voice asking you to press "1" for whatever and press "2" for something else. Pressing "0" got me nowhere. So I pressed number "4" to get to sales. That should get a human, right? Get a human it did. Appliance Repair Guy himself answered.

We chatted a bit; it was very cordial. He admitted that now just wasn't the right time. He went on to explain issues with his employees.

A few more boo-hoos, and our call was all done.

More than three years later, Appliance Repair Guy is still just a company with an owner, a lazy tech, and a revolving door of office administrators.

> *"Business and human endeavors are systems... we tend to focus on snapshots of isolated parts of the system, and wonder why our deepest problems never get solved."*
> -Peter Senge

The point of all of this is that you simply need to make the decision. Take the leap. Start your business, add an employee, buy a truck, get the software, whatever has been plaguing your mind for the past few days, weeks, or months. Just do it. Or decide it's a non-issue and let it go.

More businesses have been slow to grow because slow decisions on the part of their respective business leaders. How guilty of slow decision-making are you? Start something today. Commit to getting your business rolling or rolling faster. You got this!

The Path I Made
by Kennedy Turner, Blueprint Events, LLC
blueprinteventsllc.com

I have always been known as the person who "brings people together." Growing up, I was never the smartest kid in the class, but I was the kid who loved public speaking, meeting new people, planning events, and trying new things. After graduating college, I moved to California and worked for the regional Chamber of Commerce. I was heavily involved in planning economic development events and helping design an international award-winning program called the "Business Walk Series." This program allowed me to meet and talk with hundreds of business owners. This was when I first thought, "I should start my own business." When I moved back to Wisconsin, I started planning events full-time for another regional chamber. I knew this position would allow me to build a strong network and plan a variety of different types of events. To date, I have planned over 150 events with attendance ranging from ten people to over 1,000 people. I love that event planning is different every day, that each event is unique, and that there is a feeling of accomplishment at the end.

In 2015, I decided to jump into this crazy world of entrepreneurship. Blueprint Events, LLC is located in

Madison, WI. I specialize in business and corporate event planning throughout Wisconsin for small to mid-sized businesses as well as city economic development departments. I design events to reflect a company's culture, brand, and image.

I chose entrepreneurship because I wanted to build a business from the ground up and create a more flexible lifestyle for myself and my family. I have learned that although I am the only employee of Blueprint Events, it takes a village. I have leaned heavily on mentors and my family for support and advice. A mistake I made early on was thinking I could do it all alone. Running a business is hard. With that said, I truly believe that "an arrow can only be shot by pulling it backward." So when life is dragging you back with difficulties, it means that it's going to launch you into something great.

Share your stories:
coach@drawincustomers.com

Chapter 6

And how!

Once you decide to start your business, you need to accomplish a few simple things. Well, "simple" may be a bit misleading, but they'll seem simple after it's done. These steps may feel overwhelming, but just remember they're not that big of a deal. While it's true that only about 10% of all businesses make it to five years, most of them make it past day one.

Find a Name

I would not recommend using your name in your business. Let's lay the reasons out here:

Google "Mike's Plumbing" online. How many do you see?

Now, pretend you are a customer of Mike's and you need to find a phone number for Mike. Or make a complaint. Or pay a bill. A confused customer rarely buys.

Have you ever had anyone mispronounce your last name? If they mispronounce your last name, what are the chances that they'll spell your last name correctly? Imagine a potential client trying to find you on the internet, but failing to because they spell your name wrong.

1. Suppose I want to find a plumber. On a scale of one to five, with one being terribly unprofessional and five being a shining example of professional, how professional is "Mike's Plumbing" vs. "Leak Free Plumbing"?
2. Suppose I want to sell my plumbing business… to a guy not named Mike.
3. Suppose I want to expand my business to another region. This region happens to have a guy named Mike. This Mike also does plumbing.
4. Suppose I want to give people confidence in my name.
5. Suppose I want to be memorable.
6. Suppose I want to be easy to find online.
7. Suppose another Mike who also happens to be a plumber is not paying his bills.

> **"I wanted a global company, so I chose a global name."**
> -Jack Ma

The list goes on and on. Don't get me wrong, plenty of successful businesses have used their own names—Ford, Chevrolet, Budweiser, and Dell are doing fine. They also have a ton of cash to throw at advertising to get some name recognition.

You want to name your company for your clients, not necessarily for you. You want to name your company for how people will find you, pay you, refer you, and remember you. Can you imagine starting a car company called Chevrolet with only a few hundred bucks to spend on advertising? You better make an awesome car with a name like that.

> *"Not only is a good name catchy and memorable, it should help people understand what your business does. If your name reflects your products or services you'll have a much better chance being found via Google search, so it's important to choose wisely."*
>
> -Lori Greiner

Create a Business Entity

Putting aside the whole "corporations are people" political arguments, you want to create your own business entity. This is for your financial protection as well as for other matters relating to selling or handing off your business. You'll be starting either an LLC, an S-Corp, or a C-Corp. I won't delve too deep into the differences here. Hundreds of other books touch on what to do in that regard.

If your state makes it easy, I'd say grab an LLC for now and figure out what you really need to be later, after you're all set to open your doors. Many states allow you to form an LLC for only a couple hundred bucks and about ten minutes online. With an LLC, you can start the process of building a border between you and your business. You want your business to play in its own sandbox, so you can play in your own sandbox. That way if someone trips in your company's sandbox, they'll go after your company and not you.

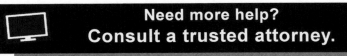

Need more help?
Consult a trusted attorney.

Lessons Learned: Keep Your Sandboxes Separate

To avoid getting your personal life mixed in with your business life from a liability point of view, it's best for you to create a legal entity for your business. As with most things in the legal world, thinking things are separate and actually documenting them as separate are two distinct things. Treat your business like a piece of real estate. Without a deed showing who owns it or that it even exists, it probably does not exist. Or if it's proven to exist, you do not own it. Unless you are liable. Then you're totally the only owner.

So, how do you keep your sandboxes separate? You need a separate checking account, savings account, credit card, and loan (if needed) for your business. If you fail to do that and someone happens to trip on your sandbox, you're at risk of what lawyers call "piercing the veil." That's lawyer-speak for having to pry your wallet open to pay for damages claimed by some clumsy sandbox walker.

Build a Professional Team

1. **Lawyer.** Find an experienced, smart, easy-to-talk-to, relatively affordable business lawyer. I have some rules for finding the right lawyers. I need to trust them, and they must be well-known in the community. That way, if they mess up, their reputation is at stake. I need them to bill fairly and to have a live human answer their phone to help with things like scheduling. I don't need to pay $500 an hour for a lawyer to navigate their calendar around their kids' soccer games. I need the lawyer to be able to talk with me quickly, confidently, and intelligently about any legal issues I may face. Lastly, I need concrete answers. I've run into many lawyers who give wishy-washy responses; when I ask a question, they talk circles around the issue and

fail to give an answer. In law, you typically need a concrete answer, because you need to make a concrete decision or take a concrete action.

2. **Accountant.** I tried to do my taxes once on my own. I thought, how hard can it really be? I sat down, made it past my name and number and started collecting paperwork. Then I hired an accountant. I happily paid them and went about my business. You may be different and you may do your taxes on your own just fine, but I don't recommend it. You want a professional to protect you from yourself. Taxes and liabilities are often gray and murky areas. How you interpret some tax code may or may not be in alignment with how the IRS interprets it. If you ever get audited, you'll want an accountant who can assist you in solving the issue. Going to an accountant after you have a mess and a headache is not advised.

3. **Banker** (or Credit Union-er). You need a good relationship with a banker or, more specifically, a commercial lender. Sooner or later you'll need money. Maybe you'll be able to float your business for a time, but at some point, you're going to need a line of credit (LOC) or some cash to buy a building or help you grow in some other manner. Money is a tool, and banks and credit unions can provide access to that tool. I will warn you that many bankers come and go. They hop from bank to bank, and you'll watch as your relationship fizzles to nothing with each career move your banker makes. So the relationship is often with the institution rather than specific bankers. Just keep networking and get to know the commercial bankers who are movers and shakers in your area.

4. **Team of Advisors**. This is a fancy way of saying smart people to ask questions. Maybe your friend down the road has a business. Maybe you find people who you can bounce ideas off through networking. Maybe you hire a business coach (like, ahem… Draw In Customers). However you do it, get a

team of advisors you can trust. It also doesn't hurt to have a team that's open to seeking support on their own issues with you. All small businesses come across similar issues. Also, give each of your advisors a copy of this book, because BOLD Business!

 Lessons Learned: You Are Only as Good as Your Team

I paid for an attorney to help me with a partnership agreement that came with a hefty price tag. I received an agreement that was so cookie-cutter that it still had the attorney's previous client company's name throughout the document. This attorney sold me a used document. Can you imagine this carelessness in a court battle? Welcome to Loophole Technicality City, Population: You.

After you get your business rolling, you should know about the next levels. This is the ladder you are considering advancing up. The levels range from "owning a job" to ruling the world. Please do not be afraid to rule the world. I am certain you would do a fine job of it.

Levels of Being an Entrepreneur
1. Self-Employed: You are the job owner.
2. Manager: You plus employees.
3. Owner: Profitable business that works without you.

The difference between these levels comes down to how much the company needs you and how much the company works for you. For example, if you are self-employed, don't have employees, and you get hit by a bus, you have a problem. The bus took your left leg, a few weeks of recovery time, and your business … all in one fell I-forgot-to-look-left swoop. This is Level 1, self-employed.

As a self-employed business owner, you are essentially the

business. If you went away, even for a day, the business would not exist. You have no one answering calls, responding to e-mails, or performing any work that nets you any income. If you were hit by this bus, your business would go away with little to no fanfare.

Suppose this bus hits you when you are the owner of a business that works without you. That same bus will still hurt you and take some recovery time (and maybe your leg). But your business will keep humming along and continue to provide you with income.

Outside of hating busses, what would your stress level be in the first scenario? How about the second scenario? Now suppose you end up in the middle. You have employees that rely on you, and the business needs you, and the bus comes along, and POW!

With a small business that is run by a manager, you have your people and processes running the business. This is Level 2, manager. Often your business is able to run without you. At least for a little while. You can go on vacation or meet with clients for a few days, and the business doesn't skip a beat. You may have a stack of messages to return and paperwork to finish. If you are hit by a bus, your business would likely survive, presuming your employees stepped up. (This last bit is based purely on your employee knowledge, engagement, and your previous trust in them.)

What happens to your employees' livelihoods in either case? If you don't care about your employees, set this book down and slap yourself. Your employees are the lifeblood of your business. They trust you to provide for them as long as they perform the tasks you hired them to do. They've kept up their end of the bargain. Your failure to yield should not cause them the need to start looking for a job.

So from a street-crossing perspective and just about every other metric, it is best to be a business owner. Of course, a business cannot typically skip the preceding levels. Most business owners end up at Levels 1 or 2 and dream of Level 3 for at least a little while. In an ideal world, you should do all you can to get to

Level 3. This is business nirvana—for yourself, your family, your employees, as well as your clients, vendors, and the eventual sale of your company.

Many companies that are valued in the billions have a CEO or founder that is essentially still a manager. If they leave, the business may not go away, though it may suffer a loss. Not every business is meant to create a passive income for you, but it wouldn't hurt.

When you're a true business owner, you're not needed. As in, ever. You make your money off of other people's work because you built up a business that allows you to not need to contribute. That does not mean that you do not contribute. What it means is that if you were hit by a bus, there would probably be a fancy funeral, but most people would leave early because your business needs to keep rolling.

Does this mean that if you're self-employed that you are going to have some problems? Well, yes. But everybody has problems. Your problems may be limited in scope until you need to bring in new clients or be in five places at once. Some self-employed small business owners are just fine being the one-person business. I'm certainly not suggesting that there's anything wrong with this, but I am suggesting it is limited in boldness. Owning a job is not ideal from my point of view. Owned jobs are good for consultants, though most good consultants have other income outside of their consulting business. This allows the consultant to do as he or she sees fit when he or she wants to.

Level 2, manager as a business owner, is actually very common. This has its pros since you're bringing in multipliers, typically employees or subcontractors. But it also has the con of creating the necessity to support your employee base. Employees typically get paid regardless of how busy a business is. But that in itself is a very small con, wouldn't you say? Employees are your company on many levels. Having employees is moving you away from trading time for money.

> " *"Any business plan won't survive it's first encounter with reality. The reality will always be different. It will never be the plan."*
>
> -Jeff Bezos

Do You Need a Business Plan?

The short answer is, yes. The real answer is yes, but not for the reasons you think. Venturing off on your own and starting a business takes a lot of time, effort, and money. It also involves risk. A business plan helps you realize roughly what you are getting into and if it's truly worth the risk. A business plan is like math homework. It may be tough to do while you're doing it, but once you have spent time on all of those story problems, you're a smarter person who is more productive without even realizing how awesome you are.

The real challenge comes where that metaphor stops. Story problems have a definitive answer. One + one = two, every time. Business plans ask you where you expect your business to be in three to five years. How are you supposed to know? You are giving a best guess. This part of the business plan is tough because no one knows what the future may bring. Not exactly, anyways.

A business plan will touch on your initial investment and what you will sell and to whom. The actual customers you get and the problems you face rarely make it into a business plan. I have rarely seen a business plan that includes a part for Things That Can Go Wrong. (Though that may be the most practical business plan ever written.)

Preparation breeds trust. You want a business plan because people who loan you money will want to know that you have a plan. It is much easier to ask for money if you have a dedicated document that states exactly what you are going to do and how you're going to do it. Otherwise you are asking people to trust you on your smile alone. How much money will people give you for undocumented potential?

And how!

"I haven't considered the results of my actions other than I am certain my business will succeed! Can I please have $50,000?"

On the other hand, business plans can be a huge waste of time. Have you ever traded stocks? Have you ever read the speculations from the experts on what stocks to buy and sell? These experts are wrong as often as they are right. Many of them are very well paid to be as accurate as the local weather forecaster. If the stock people and the weather people can't tell what the future will bring, how can anyone expect you to tell what the future will bring?

The marketing portion of the business plan is mildly entertaining as well. How much will you spend on marketing, and where will you spend this money? How many clients will that bring in? I challenge you to find anyone who was able to predict with complete accuracy and consistency what marketing did for their business without direct hindsight.

Business plans are made to appease certain people. Sometimes those people are you and your crew, sometimes those people are loaning you money. You just need to figure out who you need to keep happy.

> "Everybody has a plan until they get punched in the face."
>
> -Mike Tyson

My advice is to use your best judgement for your business plan speculation, get the minimum plan needed for your peace of mind and your business needs, and sell as much as you possibly can. Your time is much better spent preparing and selling rather than speculating about what you will prepare and sell.

So to answer the question, "Do I need a business plan?" the answer is yes. But what we really should be asking is, "How in-depth should the business plan be?" Put together a true, multiple-page tome of a business plan if you need to borrow money. If you do not need to borrow money to start your business, do a simple plan, a one-page plan similar to The Business Model Canvas (search this term in Google images to get a sample). On the other hand, you may want a bigger business plan just to help you grow as an entrepreneur. Just be sure to add a portion about Things That Can Go Wrong for your own personal plan. (But it's probably best to keep that bit out of the document you give to the bank.)

Most importantly with any plan is to work out the financial portion. How many of what do you need to sell in a given time frame to be successful? How much will those items cost you to make, deliver and market?

> *"Set your business plan to win; raise the bar or you're not going to be prepared. You need to think that what you're doing will make you $100 Million."*
> -Swiss Beatz

As a side note, business plans are very entertaining to read about three to five years after you've written them. You see what dreams you had and the nightmares you hadn't expected. Maybe you will find yourself in a completely different place. I have yet to meet a business that stuck to the original business plan to the letter. Looking back on how far you have come is great to do every once in awhile. Looking back at where you thought you would be is often even more fun. For that reason alone, your business plan may be worth writing.

I teach a business planning class and routinely see students change their entire business after putting pen to paper (or fingers to keyboard) and discovering they can't or won't do what they thought they could. The beauty of the plan is the planning itself.

Lessons Learned: Planning is Step 1

One of the most challenging aspects of planning is knowing when to stop. Or at least to start taking action amidst your planning. A plan is often never truly done. You must take action on your plan for anything useful to happen.

Are You Sure?

It's not for everyone. One of the things I want to make clear in this bold business book is that entrepreneurship is not for everyone. Much like any activity that requires dedication, persistence, and drive to achieve, some people just aren't cut out for starting or running a business.

In the books Talent is Overrated and The Talent Code, Geoff Colvin and Daniel Coyle, respectively, decode the mystery of how people get good at being great. Debunking the notion that people are born with greatness, they describe how talent as we know it is truly just success that follows roughly 10,000 hours of practice and hard work. Most people are not willing to do much for 10,000 hours, aside from watching TV. Unfortunately for couch potatoes everywhere, TV watching does not pay that well.

Why start out with a business partner instead of going it alone?
by Mason Tikkanen, Motus Financial
motuscc.com

The grass is always greener.
I think it's fair to say that most people who start businesses by themselves periodically wish they had a business partner to bounce ideas off, hear differing perspectives, or even just to simply have someone else to talk to. It's also fair to say that most people who start businesses with one or more partners occasionally wish they could make decisions more quickly, their way, and with fewer approvals necessary to move forward. But

both approaches are equally as valuable as frustrating.

My business partner and I were fortunate enough to start our business having already worked together for over a decade. We had the advantage of being familiar with each other's communication style and work ethic, decision-making approach, and client service philosophy. This was a huge advantage that not every partnership has when starting out.

Why, oh why, didn't I take the BLUE pill?

Most people don't choose to leave a comfortable salary, vacation time, benefits, and stability to have that all disappear the next day. I've seen someone compare entrepreneurship to jumping off a cliff and trying to build your airplane before you hit the ground. You'd have to be a lunatic, right?!

But, sometimes you don't recognize the place you're leaving behind. Sometimes the direction they're heading in no longer resonates with who you want to be. We decided to start our firm in order to take our skills and attempt to help as many businesses as possible, in the way we felt was most fair for all parties. We felt we had the necessary expertise and vision to fill a growing gap our industry was creating. We felt we could also find a way to support our families and future employees by filling that gap. That's why we decided to start our business.

This is to say that starting a business is tough. You will need some insane persistence. You'll have people tell you why it won't work. They'll kick and grab to prevent you from reaching success. You'll have to power through all of this. That's one of the reasons business owners are so prideful. If you had any idea what they had to tolerate and sacrifice to get the success they have, you would understand.

And how!

Like the basketball player that makes the winning three-point shot, success may only be evident to others for mere seconds, but it took years to perfect. Sweat and toil are the name of the game in sports, business, and just about any other success that is worth achieving.

My point is that maybe this isn't for you. If it isn't, you will know it. How? Simple. You will be reading these last few paragraphs and wondering, "Who is this guy talking to?"
We need to weed out those who won't be willing to tolerate the challenges of business. If you can't tolerate a little challenge in a book, what happens when your mom challenges you about your business?

> *"Many people start a business only to make money. Just to make money is not a strong enough mission."*
>
> -Robert Kiyosaki

Do the Math

I recently taught a class on what it takes to start a business. I talked with some of the students about their business ideas and started doing some math. One woman wanted to make candles. So we went through what it would cost to make them, what she could charge for them, and how many candles she could make in the time she was willing to work. Then we added in time for selling, dealing with customers, and all of the gritty details that come up when you are selling something you manufacture. Her tone went from giddy to a little concerned to throwing her hands up and claiming that maybe it wasn't for her. Realistically, she could get the business to work, but the thought of working more than 20 hours per week and every weekend in the summer at craft fairs dragged her down. Her spirit was broken in a matter of minutes.

You'll need the drive to overcome challenges like these. You need the determination to stand up for what you believe is the right business for you and say, "How can we make this work?"

Then you are one step closer to getting your business rolling.

That's not to say that you should start a business that is clearly not economically viable. Maybe this candle thing wouldn't work for her. Maybe she needs to find a different product or a twist on her initial product. Or change how she sells them. Whatever the case, starting a business is where the drive needs to be. The passion for your specific product or service should not prevent you from altering your business model to make certain your business can be successful. This should not be an all-or-nothing affair.

Can you imagine a potential entrepreneur all fired up to start a typewriter repair company? This guy could be the best damn typewriter repair technician in the world. He just has a very limited market. An uphill battle is eminent. I would recommend picking your first business to be one with a slightly shallower slope. Get a business rolling that can sustain you while you chase other dreams or offer you the time to find other dreams to chase.

How many successful businesses do you see around that are needed, but unlikely to have been someone's dream? I see dry cleaners that seem to be doing very well. If it's your dream to start a dry-cleaning business, fire away. I just doubt it's a popular dream. When I see a dry cleaner's shop, I presume that the entrepreneur saw a need, had some skills, and got that dry cleaning business rolling. For some business owners, what business they start doesn't really matter. Their reasons for being an entrepreneur can often be supported by non-glamorous businesses.

Through all of this you need to identify your passion. Is it owning a business or owning a specific business? Most small business owners eventually do not care what it is they are selling. Sure, they want to make the world a better place and make some money doing it. The drive, however, actually rests in creating a successful business, not necessarily a successful business that fits another passion of theirs.

I started a printer repair business as my first true entrepreneurial adventure. Printer repair wasn't my passion. I was simply good at it, and people loved me for my skills. After a few years of dealing with the business portion of fixing printers,

I started to get the seven-year itch. My passion was in owning a business, not in fixing printers.

It was great, though. Because this led to innovation. I created another business to feed my entrepreneurial spirit. The business I started, Calls On Call, was not even an idea when I had started my printer repair business. If I had a passion for fixing printers, I would have stayed with it. But, my passion for printers left the day I sold my printer repair company, or arguably, a few days (or years) before.

Sure, you need to have passion for what you do. You need to do what you do with the drive and confidence to thrive and survive. It is OK for the drive and confidence in your specific business to be shallow if your drive and confidence run deep in having a successful business as a whole. The downside of having passion for your specific business instead of a passion for business in general is that you may try to keep sinking ships afloat, even if it's best they just sink. You may lower prices to keep market share or try to appease customers that are unable to be satisfied. You will destroy your business from the inside out if you don't let it evolve.

Did you know that 3M started out by selling the mineral corundum to manufacturers of grinding wheels? It was not until later that they started focusing on innovative new products. The evolution of a business is necessary in any business you may start. Innovation cannot happen when you are focused on keeping what you have. Butterflies cannot exist without first being caterpillars.

Here's simple checklist for starting your business. It's not meant to be exhaustive, but it'll get you started. Check it out:

The One-month Checklist (in no particular order):

☐ **Create a name for your business**. Make it memorable and have it explain what you do. Clever is good, clear is better. Keep search engine optimization (SEO) in mind with your company name as well. Utilize the web to make sure your company will not be confused with other companies.

- **Get a website domain name**.
- **Get a logo**. From your graphic designer friend, from fiverr. com, or some other source. I would avoid clipart, though it may work as a placeholder if you need one.
- **Create a separate business entity** such as an LLC or S-Corporation. I like to start with an LLC, you can always change later. In many states, they are brutally simple to obtain. You can often find your state's Department of Financial Institutions website and create your business entity for less than $200. Typically, you do not need to work with a lawyer for something this simple, though you certainly can. Some websites claim to create an LLC for you for a lot of cash. They are unnecessary to use. Start with your state's website. Use your company name without the LLC as Doing Business As (DBA) in all of your public marketing to make changing it to a corporation later easier.
- **Create a website**.
- **Get an email address**. something@yourwebsite.com is preferred. No gmail, hotmail, AOL, etc.
- **Get a business-specific phone number**. Cell phone, Google Voice number, anything will do. Just make it different than your personal number.
- **Get an EIN number** (Employee Identification Number). This is like the social security number for your business. No lawyer needed, just a simple online form from the federal government.
- **Create a state tax ID number**. No lawyer needed, typically just a simple online form found on your state's department of revenue website.
- **Get a savings and checking account** for your business in the business' name.
- **Get business cards**. The more professional looking, the better.
- **Create a written partnership agreement** (if in a partnership). You can find basic ones online. This should cover all of the

if/then scenarios, such as if one of you wants out, then this is how they get out and what money (if any) changes hands. Keep in mind this is easy now. When your business involves 40 people and has revenues in the millions of dollars, things can get hairy. Make sure this agreement covers future growth. It should also cover divorce, death, disability, and inability to perform from either party. Basically, you get this document put together now so you have the ground rules to play nice and fair together later.

- **Sit down and talk with your significant other**. Get their feedback. Let them know this is important to you. You need their excitement, advice, and help. You can do without, but running a business isn't easy on relationships. Ask me how I know...
- **Create a business plan**. It does not have to be an 80-page dissertation. Just a simple layout of what you will do and how you'll make money doing it.
- **Get your social media buzzing**. Set up YouTube, Facebook, LinkedIn, Twitter, etc. Content can come later; you just need the channels in place, ready for content.

> "*Marketing and innovation produce results; all the rest are costs.*"
> -Peter Drucker

- **Talk money**. Who puts in what and when, and who has control over the money? Add this to your operating agreement (may or may not be a separate document). Also discuss pricing for your services and/or products.
- **Celebrate your creation**. Seriously. Go out to dinner with your families and take a couple hours to bask in what you have done. Then get back to work.
- **Hire your people**. If you need employees, the time to find them is before you actually need them. Good people can be hard to find.

All of this combined should take only a few days full-time or a couple of weeks if you pick at it a few tasks at a time.

If at any point you are feeling jittery or like it's not is a good move, verify your commitment now. What is challenging you? Nobody wants to hear, "I never really wanted to do this!" after a business is heading south. You need to be fully committed. Commitment will make you successful. Because with that commitment, you will take action. Actions get results. No action, no results.

Understand that, in business, your unnecessary empathy may slow you down. Just like Tom Hanks said in A League of Their Own: There's no crying in baseball. There is no crying in business. Be prepared for that.

The Six-Month Plan (in no particular order):

☐ **Get what you sell ready to sell.** You can get that stuff going now. This part will take some time and may never truly be finished. As in any career, you will keep refining and polishing and adding and subtracting and, well, you get the point. Trademark if needed.

☐ **Get a place to do your work**, make your product, and/or sell and distribute your stuff.

☐ **Tell your world.** Tell everyone: friends, family, coworkers, acquaintances, the mail person, the checkout clerk. Everyone you come into contact with should be told about your venture. You do not know who knows who. The main lead generators could come from your plumber.

☐ **Don't fall too deep in love with your business.** If you realize it's not a viable business, you must be prepared to walk away and start something new. Remember the Snuggle House or typewriter repair or the Yellow Pages? At some point, you may realize that things did not go as well as planned. Hopefully not, but be prepared to pivot.

- □ **Define your goals**, including a timeline. Where do you want to be in one year? Three years? What is your exit strategy?
- □ **Get systems in place** for smooth operations.
- □ **Start selling**. Find your market and hit it. Sell, sell, sell.
- □ **Get a mentor**, coach, accountability partner, or sounding board, someone or a group of people you trust to help guide you to where you need/want to be. Draw in Customers Business Coaching is available, as well as many others.
- □ **Celebrate your creation**. Seriously. Go out to dinner with your families and take a couple hours to bask in what you have done. Then get back to work.

Enjoy the Ride
by Siddhi

Buying an orthodontic practice was an experience filled with excitement, stress, and, beyond everything else, uncertainty. Many start their own business from scratch, and there are benefits to this option: You select your staff. You buy the equipment you want. You design the practice with your vision. But there are many benefits to buying an established business. How about cash flow? The comfort that comes with knowing that you will instantly have the income to pay back your loans rather than needing to sell platelets until your business takes off is one of the most important perks. The skeleton of the business is already in place, and although you may need to incorporate new protocols or restructure or hire and fire some staff, there is much less personal time invested into getting the business off the ground. At times I have regrets: It is hard to change the mindset of the staff, or I find much of my cash flow goes into updating the practice. Still, the pros have outweighed the cons.

The following are some tips to make the transition process more efficient.

If the seller truly wants to sell, (s)he will have a valuation performed. This is typically conducted by an accountant or a business transition specialty group. There are multiple methods for coming up with a value for the business, including capitalization of cash flow method, the market approach, the asset approach, the income approach, and many more. Research which method is best for your particular business. Hire an accountant or a business transition specialty group to review the valuation. Ask the accountant or specialty groups for references and contact those references. Get help, and be willing to pay for it. Make sure they are good advocates for you.

Visit networking groups months before you buy a business. Since you will need the assistance of multiple professionals including a lawyer, an accountant, a financial consultant, and a commercial lender, use networking meetings as an opportunity to informally interview people. Make sure the professionals have experience with your specific type of business transition. When buying a business, you will have a checklist of over 100 things to do. Find the right people to help you, and they will communicate with each other and take care of the majority of the checklist for you.

Set a timeline for the transition and a maximum amount you are willing to pay. If the seller seems to be "wheeling and dealing" or dragging their feet, walk away. Either they are not truly interested in selling the practice, or if they are, they will return to you on your terms.

Remember, money can often bring out the worst in people. This does not mean the seller is a bad person.

This does not mean you are a bad person. But in a business transaction where hundreds of thousands of dollars may be on the line, you become your biggest advocate, and it may get ugly. Try to detach from your feelings and think logically. Play chess before you go into the negotiations—think through as many scenarios as you can and have a plan of action for each.

Buying a business is an adoption—the seller is handing you their baby, and you are getting everything you always wanted, but have no idea what to do with it. Just remember, you will learn, adapt, grow, and above all mold that practice into your dream. Your baby. And one day, you will share that baby with someone else. Enjoy the ride.

Chapter 7

Stash the cash before you crash

66

"The best things in life are free. The second best things are very expensive."

99

-Coco Chanel

A major reason people start their own business is to earn more money than a typical job might allow them to. The ability to earn more income is one pathway to freedom, freedom to be in complete control of one's time, money, and effort. In theory, this freedom leads to happiness. When a person has a lot of money and a lot of time, it's assumed they feel happy.

Let me ask you a question. Have you ever told people you were an entrepreneur, and they assumed that this meant you had a huge yacht and an exclusive golf club membership? This is pretty sweet because it gives you something to reach for. But it can also be a challenge, because business owners may be ten years into their business but still have trouble paying payroll.

In business, money is what makes the world go round, so you better have a good understanding of it. If the words profit and loss don't mean anything to you, they should. Let's explore the money details of business.

> *"Don't stay in bed. Unless you can make money in bed."*
>
> -George Burns

Cash Flow

In 2006 I started my first real company. It was a business that made some decent money and offered some great interactions with interesting customers while giving me the opportunity to work with my hands, which I love. It brought together everything I thought I wanted.

Then reality set in. At first, there were some cash-flow issues. A bunch of customers owed me money, and I didn't have much in the bank. Since I couldn't pay my mortgage or employees with the hope of people paying me, there was a little sweating and a few sleepless nights on my end. Money in the bank trumps money owed to you.

As a side note, when you offer people net 30 terms, they often use the entire 30 days. Some even push to a few extra days past. It's difficult if you don't have a ton of cash in the bank before you open your doors.

Lessons Learned: Let the Cash Flow

Cash flow is not just a meaningless phrase used by accountants. Cash flow is the lifeblood of your business. The cash gap between cash going out for products you sell and cash coming in when those products are sold can kill an otherwise successful business. Plan for what success will cost you in the short term so you can thrive in the long term.

A wise businessman described a fitting analogy of cash flow. He said having cash flow is like standing in the middle of a river. Water rushes toward you, then immediately away from you, and every once in awhile, you get to dip your fingers into that river to get your fingers wet.

That is cash flow. The better you are at business, the more you get to dip your hands in the river. If you are really good, you bring a bucket. If you're a master business person, you set up a whole tributary system to feed many buckets.

The main idea is that if you want to stay in business, even in dry times, you need to make sure you have some water behind a dam at your bank.

Business ebbs and flows all the time. With enough money in the bank, you can ensure being able to cover your payroll, vendor costs, and any mistakes you make along the way. This is in addition to whatever other expenses are common in your business.

Another very smart person once said, "entrepreneurship is defined as making enough money to afford your mistakes." Truer words have rarely been spoken.

Essentially, you can never have enough money in your bank to cover the costs of doing business, especially with business growth on your mind. From a practical standpoint, you can shuffle the money around as needed. You can put the money in different buckets as needed. Always remember that a lack of capital has destroyed more than one great business. Well, they were almost great businesses.

> *"Avoid debt that doesn't pay you. Make it a rule that you never use debt that won't make you money. I borrowed money for a car only because I knew it could increase my income. Rich people use debt to leverage investments and grow cash flows. Poor people use debt to buy things that make rich people richer."*
> -Grant Cardone

Lines of Credit

I read a story of a manufacturing company. The owner was proud to say that he had never had to borrow money to grow his company. At first that seemed pretty cool. Never having to borrow money means never being in debt. Debt is generally not a great thing. Then it dawned on me. It suddenly seemed like one of the most absurd things to be proud of. The underlying principle of success here seemed misplaced to me.

Don't get me wrong, I am all for being debt-free. However, if efforts to keep debt-free is limiting the business growth, why wouldn't you borrow some money?

The difference often exists in the perception of debt. I still find myself not taking on what I consider to be unnecessary debt because I don't like to owe people anything—money or favors included. However, money is a tool. Using somebody else's shovel to dig a hole when all you have is a spoon is just good business practice. You could use your spoon and take ten times as long to dig your hole, thereby limiting yourself in terms of what other holes you can dig. Or you can just borrow a shovel, pay some interest and get your hole dug.

One thing I recommend to many of my clients is to get a line of credit. Get your bank to guarantee you a line of credit for a few months' expenses. Do this now while the sun is shining and things look great so that if a few bad days come around, you and your business can survive. How easy will it be to get a loan to keep your business above water when the flood has already hit? You want a line of credit before you need it. All the better if you do not have to use it.

A line of credit is also great because they're essentially free. They cost you virtually nothing until you use them. It's like an insurance policy that works as quickly as you need it and costs nothing until you actually use it. How many insurance policies can say that about themselves? Well, none. Insurance policies can't talk, but you get the point.

Speaking of insurance policies, let's suppose your building

gets taken down through some disaster—fire, tornado, flood, whatever. Will the insurance company cut you a check that day to get your building back up? Even if they did, could they get you a building in a day? Probably not. You're going to need some fast cash to fill the gap between the happy and the not-so-happy days. More than one business has been destroyed by unforeseen problems and challenges ranging from natural disasters to a tanking economy.

> *"If you borrow money to make money, you've done something magical. On the other hand, if you go into debt to pay your bills or buy something you want but don't need, you've done something stupid. Stupid and short-sighted and ultimately life-changing for the worse."*
>
> -Seth Godin

Liability

It turns out that when you have something worth taking, people may look to take it. Janis Joplin claimed that "freedom is just another word for nothing left to lose." I've listened to that song countless times. Every time I listen to that verse, I interpret it differently. It expresses an ongoing challenge in our society. You can have literally nothing, or you can have something to lose. You must either be happy with nothing or happy pursuing more.

As business owners, we need to judiciously limit our liability to prevent others from taking what will be ours. We also need to limit our personal liability for actions taken by employees, vendors, or contractors on behalf of our business. You do not want to lose your house because an employee dropped a very expensive ball.

In business, this can be done with legal corporate setups such as LLC and other corporate entities. These allow you and your business to remain independent of each other in regard to liability. An experienced attorney and commercial insurance broker can help you keep your liability exposure at bay.

As stated previously, separate bank accounts, phone numbers, addresses, and all manner of entity distinctions offer a great defense against those attempting to take from your business and pursuing financial reward against you personally for a business error.

Take steps to limit your liability include getting liability insurance for your business. This insurance is rarely used though necessary to protect your business and yourself.

Lessons Learned: Keep it Separate

It's just good business practice to keep your business accounts and possessions separate from your personal. Eventually you'll want to sell or leave your business to explore other opportunities. It will be much easier to do that if you're not intertwined in your business via shared accounts.

The Growth Conundrum

When I first started my business, I had dreams of grandeur. While I had a hard time believing that my company would ever become a Fortune 500 company, I could imagine having 200 employees, a nice office, and earning enough to not have to worry about money. I also had the illusion that just about every small business owner out there had aspirations for something bigger. Once again, I was wrong.

I started Calls On Call in response to my first business's growth. I thought that it would be easy to launch a business that solved the phone-answering dilemma for small businesses. I imagined it growing from a small company into a successful operation of 250 receptionists in a matter of months.

I was excited for phenomenal cosmic growth that would scare me. Then a funny thing happened. Nothing. I set up meetings with potential clients and chatted with people while networking and found that a lot of them were just fine being self-employed job owners with no desire for growth, or at least no action taken on their part to prove they were aiming towards growing their business.

> **"Growth is the only evidence of life."**
> -John Henry Newman

This blew my mind. How could you want to have your own business and NOT want to grow? It's like the worst of both worlds. Why would you want to deal with all the pain of owning your own business and never allow yourself the freedom that it could afford you? What I failed to realize was that the freedom that I desired, they had already found. It was in a much different form for them, but it was how they interpreted the word freedom. Freedom, to me, includes working much less than 30 hours per week. But to them, freedom is the joy of having to work at least 70.

I had failed to realize that not every business owner shared my desire for growth in their quest for freedom. This taught me that I needed to target companies that showed signs of growth, perhaps a new employee, a new car, or a new piece of software.

> **"It is not necessary to change.**
> **Survival is not mandatory."**
> -W. Edwards Deming

Shortly after I started Calls On Call, I started to get into the teachings of Tony Robbins. I was pumped up talking with other business owners and was flooded with a passion and desire for growth. Then I was taught a powerful, real-world lesson on the myriad of other paths people can take with their business.

A client called me up and said he had to quit using our

service. He was an arborist, someone who took care of trees, someone who understood growth, at least in nature. He said he was too busy. We had helped him double his business in four months by simply answering his calls. He explained that before he used Calls on Call, he could self-regulate. In other words, when he was busy dangling from a tree, chainsaw in hand, he could not answer his phone. And when he was in his recliner, he could answer his phone.

I was in a bit of shock. I felt like a chef who was told his food was too delicious. It went against everything I was learning. How can you not want to grow your business?

I challenged the arborist and asked him if he could hire people to do the work for him. He claimed that, yes, he could hire two full-time arborists and have work for them immediately. "So, where's the problem?" I asked. He replied, "I don't want to manage people. I just want to climb trees." The arborist took my barrage of questions challenging him on his self-imposed ceiling. I suggested he give the least lucrative jobs to another arborist client of ours, who was still in phenomenal-growth mode. Charge them a few bucks for each lead. Based on the numbers, this would more than cover the costs for our service, allowing him to make more money while satisfying his potential clients with almost zero liability. That would have been a bold business move.

He surprised me even more when he claimed that when someone calls his business, they want him to be the one to take care of their tree. This is when I shifted gears into you-have-to-be-kidding-me mode. It wasn't like he was the best attorney for clients on trial for murder or the best surgeon to dig out a tumor. He cuts down and trims trees. I am sure he's a great arborist, but the level of greatness for every job has a point beyond which, if you get any better, nobody cares. For many industries, that ceiling is pretty low. The differentiator at that point for most businesses is to improve their customer service.

This arborist was under the impression that he was the best. He very well may have been, but when the best do not answer their phone, good enough will do just fine. And sometimes, the best break their leg. Even when the best is out of business, you still need to call someone to get your tree taken care of.

Why didn't the arborist want to grow? He wanted the freedom in terms of time and effort while money was clearly not a motivator. Many small business owners are perfectly chipper being self-employed, as I discussed in Chapter 6. Some businesses are designed to be that way. Think service businesses where you, as the business owner, are one of the best, and to grow in a similar fashion would be challenging.

Professional speakers, consultants, (authors...wait) or other niche service industries are tough to expand beyond the individual business owner. Other industries provide for a clear path to huge growth. Basic service trades do not have a market that cares much about skillset beyond a given parameter. These trades include: plumbers, painters, cleaners, accountants and mechanics. As one-person operations, these industries are challenging to run and even more challenging to profit from.

Can you imagine being a self-employed plumber? Hauling water heaters up and down basement stairs alone, being on call 24/7/365, and keeping a decent size inventory to cover typical service calls would be brutal.

The economies of scale for a given business should be researched to figure out what size is the ideal size for your business type. This should be researched prior to the start of your business. The big question is, "Can your definition of freedom be supported by the business you want?" If not, would it make more sense to find a similar business that can scale closer to what you prefer?

For example, a restaurant can only support so many tables, customers, and orders. Beyond a given limit, something will have to give, be it capital, customer experience, or the owner's sanity. The size of any restaurant is finite. That is where multiple locations can solve the growth issue.

Let's consider a hypothetical computer company. They can only repair so many computers locally. Their territory only has so many computers in use, and only a proportion of them may ever need repair. Furthermore, the company's technicians only have so many hours available to repair their client's machines. If this company sought growth, they may need to branch out to repairing computers remotely or off-site in order to expand.

One challenge in growth that the self-employed complain about is employees. For your business to reach at least Level 2, you will need employees; they are a must. Otherwise, you'll need subcontractors, but for this argument, they are essentially the same thing. Everyone has baggage, but employees seem to bring truckloads. Anyone that has ever had employees understands a reluctance to hire. The problem is that you cannot do it all, not if doing it all includes growing your business beyond just you.

The arborist did not want to manage people, and I completely understand why. Managing employees is unnecessarily tough. It should be easy, but it isn't. Fortunately, the value of a great employee far exceeds the baggage they come with. And your growth limitations are eliminated when you start hiring employees.

If you won't take on employees, it's recommended that you at least outsource what you can. This will allow you to get more done with the underlying intention of ultimately attaining more freedom, however you define that.

Beyond employees and contractors, there may be other types of multipliers that you can seek for your company to thrive. Check out Chapter 11 for more on multipliers.

What I typically see when I speak with business owners who do not attempt growth is fear—fear of failure, fear of success, even the fear of acknowledging that maybe, just maybe, they don't know it all. People who start businesses often have pretty decent-sized egos. Admitting that someone else may know more than they do on a given topic may bruise that fragile ego a bit more than they're willing to accept.

Bold business owners face fear. They continue onward and work towards the growth that their business demands, regardless of the fears they have. Acknowledge your fears and move on as if they were a contrail high above you.

 Lessons Learned: Your Ego is Often in the Way

Many people believe that they, and only they, can do what it is they do. The bottom line is that anybody can be replaced. Use this fact to grow your business instead of growing your job.

How Much Should You Have in Savings?

According to the accountants I've spoken with, there is no hard-and-fast rule for savings in business. Generally speaking, accountants like to see that you have one to three months of operating capital. However, in the case of bold business moves, sometimes you need a lot of money to make changes. Buying a building, a machine, or venturing into a new market can cost a lot of money. Jumping on a sweet deal within your industry can also require some easy access to cash.

The challenge is to be careful about where you have all of that money. You want the money to be fairly fluid so you can make your move when you need to. But you also want that money to be earning some interest to keep pace with or hopefully outrun inflation. A money manager or fiduciary who is schooled in these areas would be a great asset to have in your pool of advisors.

I recommend a solid month of cash in reserve in a simple savings account or money market fund that has a checkbook. That way, if it's Friday afternoon and the deal of a lifetime shows up, you can make a move. This also ensures that you can still make payroll if the last deal you jumped on failed to deliver the success you hoped for. Outside of that, I like to have a few extra months of cash in a stronger interest earning account. This allows you to make a down payment if you need to show seriousness on Friday and get the rest of the cash in the days after you have signed and committed.

> "Business is a money game with few
> rules and a lot of risk."
> -Bill Gates

Who Gets a Bill?

All of this bold business growth can lead to a few issues in regards to collecting money, as mentioned earlier. Here is a tip it took me a couple years to learn and remember:

Accounts receivable will pay you. Accounts payable are what you have to pay.

Accounts receivable are assets. Accounts payable are liabilities.

Send bills to accounts receivable.

These terms are not self-explanatory, nor do they represent their relationship to one another. Maybe they're meaningful to a CPA, but to me, the opposite of payable is not-payable. Many small business owners have asked me to clarify which account is used for what. Sending invoices to accounts payable does not do very much good in payment collection attempts. I made these rules big and bold so you can slap them on your wall near where you send out your invoices.

> "That is my principal objection to life,
> I think: It's too easy, when alive, to
> make perfectly horrible mistakes."
> -Kurt Vonnegut

Pay Your People

This is not just a nice thing to do or something you should consider. Your people need to be paid, and not in IOUs. Your people took a risk by working for you, and you are legally obligated to have that risk pay at least what you promised them.

Pay your employees. Take care of your employees. Train your employees. Keep them as happy as possible. The reward for doing so will pay dividends in the form of not having to chase and train new hires constantly as well as having a welcoming work environment. Hiring is expensive and businesses develop a personality over time.

Pay Your Vendors

Choose your vendors wisely and pay them quickly. Vendors work with many clients, most of which are probably slow to pay. As a client, you'll stick out as bold and awesome if you pay promptly. One day you may need a favor, and the vendor will probably be happy to help you since they know you pay so well.

> "I'd say it has been my biggest problem all my life... it's money. It takes a lot of money to make these dreams come true."
> -Walt Disney

Do Not Be Bullied

Another issue I've found when working with some customers was bullying, or at least, attempts at bullying. I don't mean someone stole my lunch money. I mean, for example, when a large company attempts to get brutal terms for payment. One company requested net 180! They may not have tried to take my lunch money; they just wanted to give me my lunch money six months after everyone else ate. My advice, which you're welcome to ignore, is to not allow your company to be bullied. If the potential customer needs six months to pay a bill, they've probably made some mistakes. Some of those mistakes may have been not paying their bills. You do not want to be some other company's mistake.

Your company can have company policies just like larger

companies have company policies. Just as one company may have a policy to not do this or do that, you can have a policy that does not allow you to accept this or that. Just because you are small or new does not mean you are not viable.

Lessons Learned: Big Money Can Lead to Big Problems... Sometimes.

The businesses I started and ran were very well diversified. I had many clients across many industries, so my companies were able to survive some tough times. Other businesses relied on a few big clients to butter their bread. When those big clients went away, the small businesses had to make huge sacrifices to survive, if they did survive. Beware of having only a few clients that dominate your livelihood. Make sure you can survive if they go away.

How Will Your Clients Pay You?

One other detail that I've missed with clients was to assume they'd pay me when I sent them a bill. This was foolish for many reasons. It dawned on me after I made a few money-collecting calls to clients. I had assumed they were sitting by the mailbox just waiting for my invoice to show up.

One day I received an invoice from some internet or yellow-pages directory. It was essentially an artificial bill made to look like a genuine invoice. The amount was $70. Not enough to warrant crazy concern, but still it looked weird. Way at the bottom in two-point type it admitted to being a solicitation. It took a few scans for me to realize this was an ethically challenged attempt to collect money for nothing. If a company didn't have some sort of check and balance process, it may end up sending payments to some ethically challenged companies, which could lead to some cash flow issues, among other problems.

Because of this, most companies have a way to verify invoices to make sure they have received what they're paying for. Just because you sold something to a company doesn't mean that the person you dealt with has told the check-writing people. This is why it's important to ask your client what the process for bill payments will be. Most companies have a simple process. It's possible that your invoices will be automatically paid—maybe your clients are set up to pay with a credit card with no interaction from you or them. Other companies have systems that rival the terms of getting Van Halen to play at your venue. What color M&Ms need to go with the invoice?

> ❝ **"M & M's (WARNING: ABSOLUTELY NO BROWN ONES)"**
> -Van Halen contract clause, under Munchies ❞

Measuring the Money

That Van Halen contract clause was ingenious, as you probably already know. It was meant to make certain that the people who needed to read the contract actually read it. One look inside the bowl of M&Ms and the band knew whether they were at an organized venue that understood their contractual obligations. Your business financials can use simple metrics like this to stay on top of the game with just a glance. If you had to pick three metrics to gauge how successful you are, what would they be?

One of our metrics at Calls On Call is tracking incoming call volume. This is important to our business and helps us find ways to improve our service. We have a chalkboard wall that has three simple statistics written on it daily. This gets everyone in the mindset of improving and measuring routinely. What could you measure and improve in your business?

> ❝ **"The measure of success is not whether you have a tough problem to deal with, but whether it is the same problem you had last year."**
> -John Foster Dulles ❞

Collecting Money

When I started my first business, I had to chase some money. Some clients paid on the net 30 terms I provided. Others paid on the net whenever-they-felt-like-it terms. I used to get worked up in a frenzy over a few hundred dollars. Those first dollars were important for my business to survive and to get my debts paid. This client money was my paycheck.

The principle was also a huge factor at that time. They owed me money that I earned and decided that they would rather spend that money elsewhere. In some clients' cases, this was very effective stealing.

> "*Remember, always give your best. Never get discouraged. Never be petty. Always remember, others may hate you. But those who hate you don't win unless you hate them. And then you destroy yourself.*"
> -Richard M. Nixon

Back then, I took some companies to court over a few hundred to a few thousand dollars. It took a lot of time, a lot of money, and a ton of effort. Going to court is a headache for everyone involved. I never lost a court case, yet I was rarely able to collect the money I was fighting for. What I did end up with was poison in my mind. I had hate brewing toward some just plain evil people over how I thought the world should work.

After an annoying small claims court case over $2500 that seemed to go on for months, I decided that maybe I was going about this all wrong. In this particular case, I had to pay the sheriff to serve notice to the defendant. The sheriff failed to do what I considered to be a good job in the attempts to serve the individual. I am certain they had better things to do than serve a court notice. If you want something done right, do it yourself, right?

So I went to the business when I knew they would be

open, and I served them in person myself—in front of about 100 of their customers. This embarrassed the business owners quite a bit. That wasn't really my intention; I actually didn't expect to see any customers. At any rate, it became somewhat of a fiasco, as you can imagine: me letting the customers know that the business owner was not paying his bills, the business owner attempting to stop the interruption. It cost me time and effort and, in the end, I didn't get my money. The business owner filed for bankruptcy and put a lot more energy into dancing around the law than I cared to invest in chasing the money.

 Lessons Learned: Headaches are Rarely Worth it

Aspirin is cheap, but headaches are expensive. Avoid the need to use aspirin because of silly business decisions. Sometimes the better move is just to walk away.

So how do you go about collecting money that is owed to you? Have a system in place to keep track of when money is owed, and follow up with debtors on a continual basis. Eventually you have to decide to continue pursuing or walk away. The cost of walking away is often much less than pursuing. But that's for you to decide.

Otherwise, the best solution is one that prevents money from ever becoming past due: You simply get paid before you perform the services. That way, you can withhold services until you are paid. No chasing needed.

Bad debt is such a problem in some businesses that an entire industry has been built around getting paid. Think of contractors and their lien clauses or real estate agents who get paid at closing. Do your best to close the holes that leave potential for not getting paid.

But then again, some business models don't allow this option to fly. Many service businesses have a fair amount of accounts receivable that they need to just write off as bad debt.

That's it. The time, money, and effort needed to collect some debts aren't worth it. Keep track of these clients and avoid doing business with them in the future. Even if they swear they've cleaned up their act, don't do business with them. The world goes around on the flow of money and information. They attempted to interrupt that flow.

What is the deal with accepting credit cards?
by Mason Tikkanen, Motus Financial
motuscc.com

Deal? There is no deal. It costs money, even if no one feels like they should have to pay for it. But the silver lining is that many businesses attribute accepting credit cards with increased sales of 10-15% or more. If it costs a business 2-4% to accept cards, the tradeoff should be worth the trouble. Plus, you get paid in 1-2 days and don't have to worry about bounced checks or handling cash.

If you're just starting your business and you expect less than $60,000 a year in card payments, you should find a solution that doesn't have monthly fees or minimum activity fees. Examples of current solutions include PayPal, Stripe, Square, Intuit, or PhoneSwipe that allow businesses to pay as you go. However, as sales volume grows past $60,000 a year, those starter plans can get more expensive than they need to be.

No matter how you start out, there is no shortage of telemarketers, emails, and other solicitations with offers that may make you feel foolish for not taking advantage of them. Do yourself a favor and disregard every single one of them. If you want to find a reliable provider, ask your favorite banker, accountant, or trade association. If you have no faith in any of those sources, ask another business owner in your area for a recommendation.

Taxes

It's safe to say that your bold business will make you money. Because you'll make money, you'll need to pay for some things, like roads and schools and all manner of government programs. You'll also need to pay more for just about everything. Even utilities are more expensive when you are a business.

Taxes will help pay for the services needed to keep customers and commerce flowing. Get a smart accountant and use them to help you navigate the tax code. That US tax code currently has more than 10.1 million words. That's about the equivalent of 150 books like this written in mind-numbing lawyer speak.

That's the way the world works, so the solution is to make enough money to afford it. Don't hate money. Use money as the tool that it is.

Beginning and Running Your Business
by Janet Durow, Sorge CPA
sorgecpa.com

In owning and creating your own business, you need help. You may know your specific business in and out, but you may not know about the financial issues that come with it. Get expert advice before you start and as you move forward.

Some of the biggest mistakes I have seen owners make have happened at the start up. Just like the saying, "it is easier to build a strong child than to repair a broken man," the same is true in the startup of a business. It is harder to fix things after they have been started poorly than to just set it up correctly in the first place. Believe me, there are still mistakes to be made along the way, but starting your business up without help is a mistake.

Start any new business as an LLC. This is not a tax status, but a legal status. A new business should be an LLC taxed as a sole-proprietorship (or partnership if more than one owner) first, then as it becomes more profitable, as an S-corporation to save on self-employment tax. Other entity selections could be made, but you should consult your accountant or CPA.

Here are things you should get expert help with and these should be done in this order:
Select the appropriate entity type
Set up your business as an LLC
Obtain an EIN from the IRS

Here are some great tips to follow when starting up that you can do on your own:
Get organized. Keep all of your receipts and organize them by category (office expense, rent, etc.). Separate personal and business banking. Use excel or accounting software to record all expenses, income, banks, loans, etc. by month.

If you use your personal car, keep a written log of all your mileage, both business and personal. You can use a notebook or a phone app to track this; either type is usually acceptable by the IRS in case of an audit. Start with the miles on the vehicle on January 1 and end on December 31; log all work-related miles.

Open a separate bank account for the business. This goes a long way toward making you look more legitimate in the eyes of the IRS and makes tracking business expenses much cleaner. Do not mix personal and business accounts.

Get a new credit card dedicated to business expenses. If possible, try to get a small business credit card—you normally get a nice summary document at the end of the year to help with tax filing.

(Optional) Schedule a pre-filing appointment with a

CPA in late November or early December. The primary advantage to doing this is that you'll find out where you are financially, and it makes the actual tax-prep time easier during tax season.

(Optional). Open an IRA. When self-employed, you qualify for some additional savings benefits.

I had a new client come in and tell me that he was in a partnership and that he had his whole business set up and even had a tax return from the previous year with the business on it. I reviewed the return, and it showed that he reported half the income and expenses on his return, and his partner did the same. But the problem is there was only one federal ID number, and the IRS penalized them for incorrectly filing a return. They were charged a monthly non-reporting penalty; the partnership was to file its own separate return. It was quite a mess to fix, but all could have been avoided with the proper business and tax advice. This client not only paid penalties and other fees to the IRS, but also had to pay me to clean up the mess.

Choose an Accountant Who is a Good Fit

What does a good relationship with your accountant look like? What services do you expect from your accountant? Do you have certain issues that need to be addressed immediately? How does your typical day go? How do you see your accountant helping with these issues?

These are questions your accountant should ask before they even start working with you. They should be concerned with not only the work to be done, but the relationship you desire and with making sure you are a good match to what they can provide. This is simple advice; you should like your accountant, at least in a business sense if not personally. After all, how can you work with someone you don't like?

An accountant should continue to ask good questions and inquire about your business. You should not only get tax preparation and financial statement preparation from your accountant. Be willing to pay a bit more for other services that are valuable to most businesses, such as growth and profitability analysis, and at the very least, tax planning each year to help reduce your tax liability.

You Should Have and Understand Your Business's Financial Statements

As a business owner you need to know what these tell you. How much money did you make? The income statement tells you this, but if net income is high, and there is no cash flow, where did all the money go? The balance sheet can answer that; if items there do not hit the income statement as expenses, such as paying down debt or buying inventory and assets, your accountant should be able to explain this all to you.

A good accountant should also know their own limits and realize when to seek advice from another expert. Estate planning, legal issues, or set-up of employee benefit plans—these are out of the realm of most accountants, but most have contacts for this and can facilitate the communication.

Bookkeeping

A common mistake I see business owners make is in evaluating the need for a full-time or part-time bookkeeper. Do you need a bookkeeper?

Here is a scenario from a recent client. She wanted to

hire a bookkeeper because I advised her to start doing less work on the books and to start doing more to create new business. She decided that she would hire a full-time bookkeeper to do all the bookkeeping and other administrative work; she would keep me on to review, advise, and provide tax preparation. She would pay the bookkeeper $15/hr, although she wasn't sure if she would have a full 40 hours of work for the bookkeeper.

I ran the following numbers for her:

1. Full-time bookkeeper yearly cost: $31,200 ($15 x 40 hours x 52 weeks); accountant reviewing financial statements and annual tax preparation yearly cost: $800. Total yearly cost: $32,000

2. Part-time bookkeeper for mostly data entry at a yearly cost of $15,600 ($15 x 20 hours x 52 weeks); accountant for reconciliations, payroll completion, reviewing and advising, and annual tax prep at a yearly cost of $5400 ($450/month). Total yearly cost: $21,000 (savings of $11,000 from #1 above).

3. Don't hire a bookkeeper and have us do all of the bookkeeping work (data entry, accounts receivable, accounts payable, payroll, etc.) AND all of the accountant services (tax prep, financial advising, etc.) for $1400/month. Total yearly cost: $16,800 (savings of $4,200 from #2 above and $15,200 from #1 above).

Hiring a full-time bookkeeper may not always be in your best interest. The above scenarios do not even take into consideration other costs of an employee, such as unemployment tax or workers compensation. Unless your business is large enough and/or there is a need to have them on-site, bookkeeping does not always need to be done in-house.

Have Internal Controls

Separation of duties is the best way to have internal control. This basically means to have different people in charge of different aspects of your cash and assets. For example, the bookkeeper should not handle cash, the bank reconciliation should be prepared by someone who does not handle the cash, and if possible, the person who makes the deposits should not be either of those people. Make full deposits; do not take expenses out first, keep your transactions as clean as possible. Do not mix personal and business transactions. These preventative measures are more efficient than having to create a corrective system in the event of loss. It also protects your cash and assets, creates ease of processing transactions, and ensures that your financial records are accurate.

Trying to Reduce Your Tax Liability

Another issue I see is when business owners try to reduce tax liability without consideration for its effect. One common way to reduce your tax is to purchase equipment to take the section 179 deduction. While this is an option, it shouldn't be done only to reduce your tax liability. The equipment should be necessary and useful in generating income in the long run. There may be other more creative ways to reduce your liability, such as an entity change or restructure.

Overall Advice

Don't try to be the jack of all trades or wear all the hats in your business. You need to work on your business, not in it. Get professional services for financial and legal issues and hire good employees who can do the work as good or better than you. Find and keep good clients. Concentrate on building your business, and creating and maintaining worthwhile relationships with everyone you work with; consider them all your partners in business.

Watch the Money Going Out

As I write this, I have just looked over one of my company's phone bills, which has grown little by little over the years. Typically, the phone company doesn't send out simple phone bills. They prefer the ethically challenged way of dazzling or confusing you with pages and pages of what appears to be gibberish and nonsense.

I decided the phone bill seemed too high and took the time to go through it, page by excruciating page. I found a few places where mistakes and overcharges seemed to have happened. Some of these overcharges were at least two years old. One of the mistakes was a $40 monthly overcharge. That means this one mistake alone has cost us almost $1000! In addition, we had to deal with some questionable customer service from the phone company to get the charge resolved. When the customer service person tells you, "These bills sure are confusing!" you know you are in for a treat. (Apparently the phone company was not using its extra cash to improve customer service training.)

The point is that you will have to work very hard for most of the money you have coming in. Many business owners let the money flow out to reputable vendors that they routinely use without thinking twice. Many of these vendors have bills that are all but unreadable, even to their own people. It is best to know what you are getting in exchange for what you are paying. Especially when it comes to utilities that often make much of their money from overcharging or hiding fees for services you may or may not know you are receiving.

In 2014, the FCC fined the four largest wireless carriers $353 million for overcharging customers. In the FCC challenge, most of the carriers essentially stated that everyone else is doing it, so why can't we? It happens so often that it necessitated a word to define the practice of unauthorized charges. That word is "cramming," an industry term to describe this exact practice.

That means that many companies are OK overcharging you, and you are giving consent by paying the bill and never challenging them.

Bold business owners know how to watch the money going in as well as the money going out, and they know when they need to look at the bills they are paying. Take one afternoon every quarter to go over your bills with a fine-tooth comb to find discrepancies. You'll learn to spot overcharges easily, and eventually, you won't need so much time to do so.

The same goes for your retirement and investment fees. So many companies use confusion tactics to create a sense of resolution for their clients, basically having their customers throw their hands up and assume that their financial planners are doing the best they can for their clients.

You can use a simple rule to know if you need to spend time poring over a certain bill: Is it a regulated industry? If it is, there is a solid reason. Pay special attention to those bills.

Relationships, Money and Success
by Nicole Harvey, Kneaded Relief Day Spa
kneadedreliefdayspa.com

My partner, Duke Harvey, and I decided to purchase Kneaded Relief Day Spa in 1997 when I was only 23 years old. We started, as we call it, a breach, because we knew little to nothing about the business before deciding to purchase it. We both decided to go back to school to learn a trade in the industry, which has helped us tremendously over the years. We can better understand our team, relate to our guests, and have valid conversations about the industry and the trade.

One of the earliest stumbling blocks we came across was money. Our accountant told us, "When you hit that brick wall, let me know." We had no idea what he was talking about as it was the holiday season, and money was flowing in from gift certificate sales. We bought new equipment, remodeled the spa, gave pay raises we had no justification for, and literally spent the money in our account thinking it would keep flowing in. Well, clients started coming in to redeem their gift cards without purchasing new ones. We were running into a cash flow crisis, so we contacted our accountant. Luckily, he was able to connect us to a banker that was willing to loan us some money. We realized that not only did we spend money that wasn't ours (a gift card is not a sale until the service is rendered), but we also failed to take out enough money from the beginning to start and grow the business. Lesson learned!

Throughout the years, we realized how important it is to have a good relationship with your banker and your accountant and to not discount your services heavily.

When the recession hit, we knew we had to pull the purse strings in tightly, and because we built a culture of openness, our team knew it too. They actually told us that if they would have gotten a raise during that time, they would have looked for another job because they'd have doubted we'd be around much longer. Cash flow is king and profit is not cash! Those are the truths you must live by as a business owner.

Over the years, we have grown tremendously, yet there is always more room to grow. Last year we hired a business coach and that was one of the most valuable things we've ever done as business owners. To have someone on the "outside" looking in at your business with no bias and no ownership, creates a lot of clarity. Looking through someone else's glasses may not be the most fun thing to do, but it's definitely needed. You do not see your business as someone else does; you do not see the holes like someone else does; you do not see where you need to grow like someone else does. It helped us patch up some leaky holes and grow our business more in the past year than we have the past 18 years. We have since developed new systems that our business and our team yearned for. It has helped us to be an even more cohesive team and successful business. I wouldn't trade it for anything, even through all the hard work, sweat, and tears.

Do what you love, what you are passionate about. Balance your home life and your work life, follow your cash flow, and you will succeed!

Money is Pretty Cool

I recently gave a presentation about what it takes to start a business. When we came to the subject of money, I explicitly said that money is good. Money is a tool, and I was fired up explaining that once you have earned money, you should be proud of it. As I was spouting my opinions, I felt a bit like Gordon Gecko. You know, the whole, "greed is good" thing? The response I received from one audience member was formidable, if not a bit entertaining.

Her objection was essentially hatred towards "rich people." I'm not sure where you stand in regard to rich people. Maybe you love them, maybe you hate them, maybe you are one. (How do you even define rich? That's like defining pretty. Your pretty could be my pretty ugly, and your rich could be my flat broke. Like most things, rich is relative.)

This audience member said she wasn't interested in making too much money. She was OK making some, but not so much that it would be "noticed." As we spoke, I tried to get her to define "too much money." How much is too much?

I quizzed her a bit and asked her what would happen if, one day, she found herself a millionaire. She said she would buy a nice house. I pushed further and asked about a car. She said she would have a nice car, but nothing else. She did not want to show off. So we found the root of the problem; it wasn't that she didn't want to make a lot of money, but that she didn't feel comfortable with the world knowing that she made a lot of money. She was afraid of how her financial success would look to other people.

I recommended that when she is successful in her business and makes a lot of money, she think about all the things she can do to make the world a better place in her own way. The limiting factor for her, me, you, and every other business owner is themselves. With head trash like what she was carrying around, her business would be limited in potential. Does your business have a similar limitation?

Lessons Learned: Greed is Good

If you do not want to call it greed, call it a desire for more than what you currently have. Without that desire and that hunger, you will be limited in how far you and your business can go.

If you are planning to start or currently run a business but don't want to make too much money, you need to change your mindset. You can never make too much money. Yes, you can spend too much money, but making too much just can't happen. Until you make that ill-defined "too much money," you have no idea what you'd actually do with it. Maybe you'd be the person who sends money out to feed the world, solve a crisis, or help others in need. What is your passion? What would you love to see improved in this world? Is it possible that you could do more good with more money?

I did what I could to let these future entrepreneurs know that someday they're going to make a mistake in their business or that some unexpected setback is going to happen. A bad employee, a fire, a fallen tree, or frivolous lawsuit will come along and knock on their door. The risk these business owners are taking by not striving to make what they consider to be "too much" money is huge.

> *"Wealth is not to feed our egos, but to feed the hungry and to help people help themselves."*
> -Andrew Carnegie

Chapter 8

" *"My favorite things in life don't cost any money. It's really clear that the most precious resource we all have is time."* **"**

-Steve Jobs

My wife and I got married in 2006. We were having a blast having our own jobs, our own money, and our own time to do what we did best—work and play with a little sleeping and eating thrown in to make sure we could get up and do it again.

Around 2009, my wife decided that she wanted to have a kid. I wasn't such a fan of the idea for two reasons. First, much of the current population seem to be idiots, and I thought I would be doing this kid a disservice by bringing him or her into this world. Second, I had two businesses that consumed a lot of my time. I also lifted weights and went for daily runs to keep in shape. (I'd seen out-of-shape people, and I did not want to become one of them.) Plus, my friends with kids didn't really seem happy. "You don't know the joy!" is what I would often hear after listening to a friend's four-year-old scream bloody murder when told it was bedtime. Not my idea of fun.

At any rate, it turns out that sometimes, in the world of relationships and business, a compromise is just not possible. You can't have half of a kid. Believe me, I checked. So, since no compromise was available, I had to consider my options.

I could say no and either risk the relationship dissolving or being hated for not allowing my wife to fulfill a need that is, essentially, an instinctual desire. (This isn't over a piece of cake or a house to buy. This is a question of continuing the species.) Or I could say yes and deal with the consequences of having a child. This would mean packaging all that I have ever feared in my life and presenting it to a tiny, crying package. Alternatively, I could just leave the relationship. No chance of having a kid if I'm not in a relationship, right? This was truly the least respectable of my choices. Though if you have ever been in this predicament, I can understand why you might have considered this option.

I chose the second option. Sure, let's have a kid. As a family, we can find out how challenging it is, and I will put my life as a captain of industry on hold for 20 (or so) years. Seems like the most realistic outcome, right?

I'll save the long-winded version for another time, but we finally did succeed in having a beautiful baby boy named Max. I'll end this version by telling you the reason I brought you here: Finding out that you're having a child raises some very interesting questions that I hadn't considered before. The first real question came in the form of a challenge: How can I make this kid the best he can be?

The answer that came to mind was not "work more." The answer was—and still is—to spend as much time with him as possible. This insight came to me from my experiences interviewing for employees.

Do you know how many complete morons apply for

jobs every day? I can tell you, from my small pool, that it is a staggering number. Worse yet, these morons have parents that presumably raised them. These parents either did their best (or at least adequately enough) to allow the child to survive their upbringing. As adults, these children were now on their own. And they were really, really dumb. I did not want my son to end up in a job interview during which the interviewer thinks to him or herself in bewilderment, "Who were this kid's parents?" feeling like society, as a whole, had dropped the ball on this whole child-rearing business, as I sometimes feel when I interview morons.

Importantly, this child came to help me just as much as I needed to help him. I was working too much for far too little, and Max had to show up to tell me that. He told me by screaming and crying and hugging and playing. He needed me to spend time with him, to help him learn and grow. But this is a business book, and a BOLD one at that. So what am I doing explaining the birth of my son to you?

Simple. It doesn't matter if you have a kid, a car, a mansion, or a spouse for whom you do what you do. You need a compelling reason why you are doing it. You read books like this to get better. But what does getting better really do for you? Does it make you more money? Great—but for what? A better car? Okay. But for what? This section of The BOLD Business Book is to challenge you to ask yourself repeatedly until you have a solid answer to "Great—but for what?"

> "Work mixed with management becomes not only easier but more profitable. The time is past when anyone can boast about 'hard work' without having a corresponding result to show for it."
> -Henry Ford

Gravestones

No one ever died wishing they had worked more. Maybe people have wished they had worked better or smarter or harder, or maybe they've wished they had worked at a different job or in a different industry. But the volume of time spent at work instead of living life is likely the biggest regret any one of us could have. Can you imagine a worse regret?

> "You may delay, but time will not, and lost time is never found again."
> -Benjamin Franklin

In my case I was spending too much time at work because I didn't know any better. I thought you had to work a full day. And after that full day of work, you had to work more at networking events. And when you finally made it home, you did paperwork that didn't make sense to do while you were hustling during the day. This was a belief that just the mention of having a kid destroyed. The actual arrival of my son blew open the system that I had created and a giant hole into its hull like the iceberg into the Titanic. In my case though, the ship was strong and not only stayed afloat, but moved faster and smoother than it ever did before. Once again, this pain was my privilege. Just as much of your pain is your privilege.

 Lessons Learned: Problems or Opportunities

Challenges are only periods of growth veiled as obstacles. This holds especially true when it comes to managing and prioritizing your time.

Priorities Get Done

It seems to be time to offer the time management advice that I discovered by messing up my own schedule and failing to make deadlines. The bottom line is that if the task is important

131

enough, it will get done. You will find a way.

The basic tips for time management success that I have grown to love include bits and pieces from various sources of inspiration. Tony Robbins likes the "chunking" method. This is where you take everything you need to do and chunk it into a few key categories. For example, if you look at your to-do list and you see an endless array of menial tasks such as picking up laundry, firing an employee, paying the bills, and picking up the kids, you may feel overwhelmed. However, if you chunk those into three categories—such as work, family, and play—dozens of items become three things.

I recommend that you keep a calendar, preferably electronic and mobile, such as a Google calendar. Carve out blocks of time to accomplish your weekly and monthly tasks. For some people, the very thought of being overwhelmed is enough to get them to procrastinate. Chunking your task list brings it into a more manageable light.

I received a tip from a sales trainer I worked with. He asked if I would be late for a blood transfusion. As I said, if it's important enough, you will find the time. There are some things you just have to do and do on time. Like dialysis.

> "We are what we repeatedly do. Excellence, then, is not an act, but a habit."
> -Aristotle

Fail One, Fail All

You also have to understand the perspective of those you let down when you are late or fail to follow through on what you promise. Imagine you're five minutes late to a meeting with 60 attendees. That means that you wasted 300 minutes (5 x 60 for those without a pen) of human time capital. That is a lot of human capital. Just think how much time it would add up to over the course of all of the meetings everywhere. The point is that all of these people could be doing more valuable things than waiting for you.

One of the greatest business books I ever read was Tim Ferriss' *The 4-Hour Workweek*. It covered a few main points that really helped me with time management and taught me that not every job takes 40 hours per week to do. So create a business that takes less than 40 hours per week. Maybe even aim for four.

> *"Conditions are never perfect. 'Someday' is a disease that will take your dreams to the grave with you."*
> -Tim Ferris

Ferriss discussed two approaches for increasing productivity:
1. Limit tasks to those that are important to shorten work time (80/20 rule).
2. Shorten work time to limit the tasks to the important (Parkinson's law).

80/20 Rule

The 80/20 rule is probably something you've heard of before. (This is a business book, so I have to mention it. Publisher's rules.) It states that about 80% of your productivity comes from 20% of your actual time spent producing. 80% of your time that is wasted (I'm looking at you, text messaging and social media) could be chopped down or eliminated altogether to make yourself more productive. These are things you can actively measure. We have access to software that can do an insane number of tasks for us, data collection being of the most powerful and useful.

Parkinson's Law

Parkinson's law states that "work expands so as to fill the time available for its completion." The Parkinson of Parkinson's law is Cyril Northcote Parkinson. Cyril was writing about expanding bureaucracies, specifically in Britain around 1955. But all bureaucracies seem to follow this rule. You know the kind. The kind that suck the free time right out of your day while you wait in line at the DMV.

The reason Parkinson's law is so relevant to time management is that if you give yourself too much time to do something, you'll end up wasting time. Cut your allotted time down, and you'll be much better at finding a way to accomplish your task.

I tested this theory by taking Fridays off. I no longer work Fridays. I removed 1/5th of my entire work week to accomplish two things: 1) give myself a longer weekend to get play/home stuff done and 2) prove to myself that it can work. I challenged others to do it, so I better take my own prescribed pill. Bold business, baby!

Do you know what happened? Not a blink of an issue. Oddly, I've closed more deals with a simple five-minute phone call on Fridays (when the potential client calls me) than I close Monday through Thursday as I attempt to stoke deals up. Maybe it's because when I'm elbow deep in a hobby or home project, I don't like to get interrupted unless it's worth my time. So the conversation goes from me annoying you and wanting you to pay me Monday through Thursday, to you annoying me and you wanting to pay me on Friday. That's pretty sweet.

The takeaway from Parkinson's law is to use your allotted time for a project or task wisely. Don't give yourself ample time to accomplish anything. Put deadlines on everything. Failure to do so will make certain that your tasks absorb more of your time than they need to. Time is precious, so spend it wisely.

Measure What Works

You can install a piece of software on your computer that monitors what you do over the course of a day and lets you check out where you are spending your time. You can keep a journal and make notes every time you switch tasks. Or consider keeping a checklist on which you put a slash every time you perform some task. However you do it, exercises like these can make you aware of the time that you waste. Use this to make some changes.

I stopped watching the news. Believe it or not, my life is just fine. I'm completely out of the loop on who is famous, who was shot, or who the current scapegoat for the affairs of the world is. My life is so much more peaceful. I also seem to think better of humanity. This alone saves me at least 30 minutes a day. If I really need an update, I can get it from my friends who fill me in on what I "missed."

A friend of mine thought I was crazy for not watching the news. "You don't know about this or that?" he would ask. "Nope." I would reply, and I am very much OK with that. I asked him about the most recent news he was concerned about. "What did you do differently in your day after hearing this news? Did you duck for cover or look over your shoulder at every corner? Did you write a letter to your senator? Did you drive around fuming? Or did you go about your business as if nothing really happened?" I found that I was not altering my daily activities based on the news, so I eliminated it from my daily routine. One less thing to balance, right?

> "You just got done organizing your life. That's great. Now put some pants on and take me for a run."
>
> -My Dog

Do It For Me

Another thing I like to do for my personal time management is to have other people do my work. It's easier to prioritize if someone else has to manage the tasks and accomplish them for you. That's what outsourced professionals and employees are for. And of course, these people want to get paid. But the idea is that if I can make more money and have more fun coaching a client for an hour, why would I spend an hour adding business cards to my database? I can delegate that to an employee for a few bucks. The job gets done in a way that's better than what I could have done, and more importantly, it actually gets done.

> *"The most common way people give up their power is by thinking they don't have any."*
>
> -Alice Walker

Time Management and Tires

In order to understand time management, it helps to consider the tires on your car. Before you skip this handy metaphor, take a walk with me around your car. How are the tires looking? Some of you will note at least 6/32nds of an inch of tread and an admirable wear pattern. Others will simply see that the tires are black and round. We don't care about details here; we care about whether the tires need to be replaced. This is a yes-no question that many people can't answer until they're on the side of the road with a blown tire.

Tires are maintenance items that need to be replaced routinely. You need to make time to replace the tires. Maybe you price them out and research them online. Maybe you just schedule a time with your favorite mechanic to replace them. Maybe you trust your favorite mechanic to tell you when you need to replace them. Either way, this is proactive time management. Or perhaps you end up skipping the tire thing. They aren't that bad, right?

I worked at an auto repair shop for about 5 years. We sold a lot of oil changes and a lot of tires. I can tell you a few things I learned in regard to tires and time management.

Just about every flat tire that came to us was clearly destined for failure because they were worn out. Countless times I lifted a car up on the hoist, spun the lugnuts off, grabbed the tire, and felt the distinct sensation of hundreds of tiny steel points poking into my fingers. These wires were not meant to be exposed. Similar to the bones in your body, they are for structure, not for appearance. So when a customer would come in with tires that worn, I hardly felt bad for them. Sure, the moment the tire popped may not have been ideal. The fact is that borrowed time wants to be repaid at the most inopportune moments. It may be best to avoid borrowing time in the first place.

Lessons Learned: Borrowed Time is Expensive to Pay Back

We all borrow time in some way. We ask for favors from others, or we put off doing what we know we need to do. The best success comes from just getting the job done. Like now.

Why Didn't You Do It?

The main focus of time management should not be what you do consciously but what's happening behind the scenes within your unconscious mind. How many times do you have something on your to-do list that you just can't get done even though you are consciously aware of it? Perhaps your unconscious mind is preventing you from doing it for some reason. You need to control that, figure out why it isn't getting done, and take care of it. Your unconscious mind is the powerhouse behind true time management. Asking yourself questions such as, "What is good about this not getting done?" or "Who do I hurt if I do get this done?" may help you uncover some reasons you are not accomplishing some of these tasks.

In order to solve the most persistent time management issues, it often helps to have an accountability partner. At the seminars I host, I often invite an attendee to share their time management issues. I then ask another member of the audience, seated near them, to be an accountability partner. Their task as an accountability partner is to follow up with this time-challenged attendee in three days. All they need to ask is, "Did you do your stuff?" A simple yes or no is all that is needed. No excuses, just a yes or a no. If it's a yes, then we're all good. If it's a no, then we either have a challenge we need to overcome or we need to assess whether the task is really as important as we thought it was.

Lessons Learned: Accountability Partners Will Help You Get It Done

By getting yourself an accountability partner or group, you're inviting others to hold you to a standard that you claim you want to meet. Likewise, you do the same for them. For more information on this topic, visit www.drawincustomers.com/accountability.

Top Five Tips for Improving Your Time Usage in Business

1. Organize your stuff: your desk, your car, your house. A clear desk will help you sort through your mind. A cluttered desk will only serve to remind you of all that you have left to do.

2. Keep track of all of those crazy little ideas that show up in your head. Write them down in a little notebook or on your phone. They will serve you well someday. This list is from one of those crazy ideas.

3. Schedule time weekly to discuss your business with a mentor or accountability partner. You need someone to both keep you on task and give you the motivation to keep going. Find someone you want to impress, and impress them.

4. Say no when it does not serve you or the greater good. Be very careful saying yes. The power of no is one of the most powerful tools you have.

5. Block out time during your week to get things like email organization taken care of. Block out family time, fun time, and work time. Stick to that calendar and live a whole new level of freedom.

"The more you sweat in peace, the less you bleed in war."
-Asian Proverb

You vs. the Clock

Recently, I was running around like a crazy man getting ready like I always do—wake up to an alarm, take the dog out, feed the dog, work out, run with the dog, feed the kid, shower, shave, brush teeth, get dressed, and race out the door in an attempt to beat the traffic. Only this particular day, things were different.

One of the clocks in my house was reading 4:38. I wake up at 4:20 a.m., so I thought I was only marginally behind and moved along gradually to making stellar time. At some point I noted the clock still said 4:38. I checked the clock; it was dead. When is the best time to replace the battery in a clock? Before time stands still. My clock had become a static piece of art. It turned out that it was just an illusion that it was serving as a tool that kept me on target.

Time may be the one thing ruling our lives that we have little direct control over. Or at least, we don't exercise much control over it. I would like to illustrate a time management opportunity. The opportunity is control and decision-making ability. Allow me to explain. You are given the same 24 hours per day that everybody in this world has, right? You can use those 24 hours in productive and satisfying ways to live your best life. Or you can live with a mental attitude of procrastination.

Let's assume, since you are reading this, that you are working to be the best you that you can be. Though you may procrastinate, you see it as an issue that needs to be resolved.

Step 1: Detail what needs to get done. The keyword here is "needs." Skip the desires and the wants and go straight for the must-happens. Things like showering, dropping your kids off, and feeding the dog. You must do all of these.

Step 2: Detail what must happen at certain times. Perhaps your kid needs to be dropped off at 7:48 a.m., and you know that if you leave your house at 7:12 a.m., you slide in at the perfect moment. You have experience with your routine, though you may not have designed it. It may have just evolved on its own. Now is the time to take control of what you can.

Step 3: Set up your routine each working day so that you have mapped out what you will do and when you will do it using the steps above as guidelines.

Step 4: Plan to be early and have something to do when you are. Being on time is important and lets others know you are organized. This can help you make a sale, meet your match, or get the best seat. Time saved is time earned.

Step 5: Use your new routine and keep track of where you are with each glance of the clock. Make sure you are on target or ahead.

Step 6: Improve your routine. You'll be running late at some point, and you'll find a way to get more done in five minutes than you could previously do in seven. (Remember Parkinson's law?) If you save two minutes every weekday, you will have saved over eight hours by the end of the year. What can you do with an extra eight hours every year?

Lessons Learned: Using Every Minute

Whenever I was early for something, I felt like I was wasting time. I was available ten minutes before a meeting, and all I had was time-killing apps on my phone to keep me company. This is lost time you can never recover.

Be sure you have a book, a knowledge increasing app (Facebook is not knowledge increasing), or a notepad for you to brainstorm ideas, with you at all times. This includes stop lights, coffee lines, and waiting for others who are running late.

Step 7: Time-map before each day begins. Be like a pilot: know your destination before you get in the plane. Adapt if needed, but for the most part, your journey to the end of the day should get you the results you want. If you didn't achieve those results, you need to ask yourself one question: "What could I have done differently to guarantee that I would have achieved my goals for today?"

Step 8: Plan for obstacles. Some days, your life may be hindered by obstacles you didn't see coming. Plan for those obstacles and do what you can to prevent them. Being in a constant state of reaction to obstacles will lead to you being frantic. Frantic is not how you want to be described as a person. Instead, put procrastination to use on your worries. Worry later. Much later. Perhaps never.

> "Either you run the day, or the day runs you."
>
> -Jim Rohn

Wasn't Me

As a side note, you will occasionally be late to a meeting or an appointment. If you are late to a meeting with many people, get in and seated as quietly and quickly as possible. Do not mention your lateness unless you're supposed to speak within five minutes of arriving. Beyond five minutes, the attendees are likely to have forgotten that you were late. It will only make your lateness worse. Just pretend it was not an issue. If you do need to speak within five minutes of arriving to the meeting, apologize once and move on to your topic. No one came to the meeting to hear your excuses.

To Do or Ta-Da

Holy cow, my to-do list is huge! Every morning I throw together a to-do list, and there's about 50 gazillion things on it. Then, when I see I've only gotten three of those things done, I feel like a failure. But this is all wrong. My to-do list does not need to be that huge.

> "Every morning I walk by a funeral home, and that's my productivity hack for how to make sure your to-do list is properly prioritized."
>
> -Anil Dash

First, I should be outsourcing a lot of it. Second, the stuff I put on this list may not be that important. What if I look at this list

141

and consciously told myself I will only accomplish three of these things? How cool and how happy would I be at the end of the day? I'd look at that list, and if I accomplished only those three things, I'd feel like Fonzie. Whatever I accomplish beyond those three items was just an add-on, a little whipped cream on your mocha.

The idea is that you want to look at your to-do list, pick three—and only three—things to take on and throw your energy into. If you get those three things done every single day, whatever they may be, at the end of a typical work week, you will have gotten 15 major things done. How cool is that? We're talking extra whipped cream on that mocha.

Think about it, take it easy, one slice at a time, because getting three things done each day is superior to getting none of 50 gazillion done.

The key to excellent time management is to manage and avoid feeling overwhelmed. We all have a lot to do. The perception of it all being too much is easy to cling to. However, if you break down each item on your list to an estimate of how long each task will take, you may find you actually have a lot of leftover time. Or you'll see that it's impossible to do it all and acknowledge that you need to remove or delegate some items on your list.

You can look at excellent models of time management, like those of pilots. Check out any airport terminal board and you understand why. Yet most pilots are hardly overwhelmed. They have trained themselves to do what they need to do when they need to do it. This includes actively training for emergencies. Check out *The Checklist Manifesto* by Atul Gawand for some details on how many pilots do this.

> "*Time is a created thing. To say 'I don't have time' is like saying, 'I don't want to.'*"
>
> -Lao Tzu

Boundaries

Once you find yourself in the position of owning a BOLD business, you may find that you have some extra time. With this extra time, you may want to make the world a better place. You can do this by volunteering or helping other businesses. You can even start other businesses. But it will be important to set boundaries.

Boundaries in your calendar are rules that you set up that help you decide whether or not you want to say yes to a request. For example, at 4 p.m., I head home to play with my son. If I get a request to go to a networking event or to volunteer after 4 p.m., I rarely say yes. People understand the no and appreciate the reasons why.

I used to say yes to just about everything. I was hustling and bustling all over the place helping people left and right. I had no time for me, no time for my family, and little to show for my labors but a warm, fuzzy feeling. This is not ideal.

Another boundary can be based on location. To avoid traveling unnecessarily, it may make sense to create rules that define when and where you will travel. A business acquaintance wants to chat over coffee 20 miles from your house? Meh. Existing client that makes up 25% of your revenue wants to meet in Denver? Your bags are already packed.

Your boundaries should be designed to make time for what is important in your life, maybe working out, enjoying dinner with your family, or visiting your psychologist. The idea is that you set your boundaries before you need to consult them. Make sure the people that add things to your calendar are aware of your rules.

The calendar on the next page shows Monday through Friday with slots for additional appointments added to it. This is my calendar for a few months in the future. Fridays are blocked off, save for a few emails. Sales times, writing times, networking times, and kid times are all blocked out. The result is that when someone contacts me to meet or to help them, I can fit them in my calendar without losing my focus or running out of time.

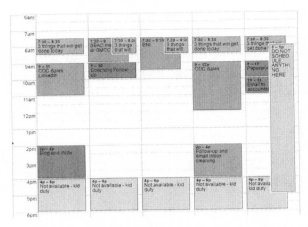

The important stuff will get done because it's scheduled. Like I tell my wife, if it is not in the calendar, it doesn't exist.

> *"If you spend too much time thinking about a thing, you'll never get it done. Make at least one definite move daily toward your goal."*
>
> -Bruce Lee

Prepare by Priming

Another tool I use for time management comes from a priming exercise I do every morning based on something I learned from Tony Robbins. I take ten minutes each day to just chill out and think. I divide the ten minutes into three pieces. Each piece is 3 minutes and 33 seconds long. I use a boxing round and workout timer app to notify me of the different rounds.

The exercise for you will go like this:

Gratitude: The first piece is to give thanks for all that you have and all that has helped you. Maybe it is as simple as a sunrise, maybe it is as specific as your neighbor's huge snow blower saving you during the last snow storm. It doesn't really matter. The point of the exercise is to thank whatever you believe in (e.g., God, Buddha, the Universe, mysterious powers that you do not understand, luck or simply fate) for bringing these things into your life. It also lets you become aware of the fact that there are forces going on around you that can alter your course. Some of those forces are very helpful. Thank them.

Energy: In this part of the session, you concentrate on your body and a sort of energy we all have. You simply imagine the energy flowing in, around, and through you. It will go from the top of your head, down through your body, and into your legs toward the floor. Then it moves back up again. It continues to flow in this pattern as you build it up within you. Once you feel really energized you think of who or what you'd like to send energy to. When this energy is triggered and milling about, you can send it out to people you want to help, things you want or need, actions you want to take. You are using this energy to bend the universe to your will. It may sound crazy at first, but the idea is that you are delivering focus to certain things. Where focus goes, energy flows.

> "It followed from the special theory of relativity that mass and energy are both but different manifestations of the same thing—a somewhat unfamiliar conception for the average mind."
> -Albert Einstein

Accomplish: In this piece, you concentrate on three—and only three—things that you will accomplish today. Maybe you have a big meeting coming up to prepare for, or you need to spend time with your kid or spouse, or maybe you need to start a business. Whatever it is, use this time to imagine yourself doing these things. Your mind doesn't know the difference between imagination and reality. Utilize this ambiguity as a tool to help you.

From time to time, you can choose to replace the last exercise with one in which you pick one or two things that you will accomplish over the next month or year. This alternative should be used as a rare deviation.

During the priming exercise, I typically listen to some basic meditation or relaxing music found easily on the internet. (YouTube is an excellent source for relaxing music.) After the priming exercise, I'm energized and ready to take on the day. I wake up at 4:20 every morning. When the alarm goes off that early, you reconsider many life choices. Over the course of getting my routine going, the time I wake up no longer matters.   After getting the dog outside and grabbing some water, I fire up the priming exercise. All of a sudden, 4:20 a.m. doesn't seem so early. Of course, you don't need to do this as early as I do, but you should do it every day. It's only ten minutes a day, so you can handle it. Try it for 30 solid days and let me know how you feel.

> "You should not be carried away by the dictation of the mind, but the mind should be carried by your dictation."
>
> —A.C Bhaktivedanta Swami

Death and Business

Recently, a friend of mine passed away. I call him a friend because if I ever went to a networking event and no one showed up but me and him, it would still be a great event.

Business friends are like that. You rarely see many of them outside of work, and there's nothing wrong with that. But every once in awhile, you come across a person from whom you know you can learn and who is willing to teach you. It just so happens that it occurs over a beer or two rather than in a classroom setting. And often, neither of you is sure who is doing the learning and who is doing the teaching.

From my experience with this loss, I cannot help but want to write some advice for you, dear reader. Take this with the grain of salt it may deserve. Live your life to the fullest. Start, run, and kick ass at your business. If you feel that you have failed, get up and try again. Life is too short to not push for a better life the entire time. Appreciate what you have earned and savor the challenge to earn more.

The journey is the success, as I and many others have said countless times before. What would you have to appreciate if everything was given to you easily?

I don't know what happens after we pass from this world. But I do know what happens while we are alive, here and now. You do too. Are you making the most of it?

It was beautiful to see how many lives my friend had influenced for the better. I'm hopeful that I'll inspire as many people to make a positive change in their lives, and I wish the same for you.

We have a responsibility to make the world a better place. To share our gifts with those around us. In failing to do so, you slap the face of whatever creator you believe in. (And I am guessing that whatever or whomever you believe created you will not be pleased with being slapped in the face.) All you need to do is enjoy the life you have been given and learn, explore, expand, and improve while you help others do the same. Can you think of anything more exciting and worthwhile than that?

Sappy time is over. It is time to get back to work. Thank you for appreciating what you have and nurturing it to grow.

> "Time, time, time. See what's become of me. While I looked around for my possibilities. I was so hard to please."
> -Simon & Garfunkel, Hazy Shade of Winter

Chapter 9

Advertising, marketing, and other black magic.

" "We need to stop interrupting what people are
interested in and be what people are interested in."
                                                    -Craig Davis
"

One of the growing pains I mentioned earlier came with navigating the world of advertising. I remember thinking I needed a Yellow Pages ad. At the time (2006-2008), Yellow Pages still existed and people still used them, at least a little. (I had some older clients, so settle down.) The internet was good and getting better. Web 2.0 was gaining momentum, but online searches for local services of any kind were not the greatest.

It was a period of transition that merited being in both the Yellow Pages and online. These were frustrating times for a business. Before the internet, there had only been so many mediums of advertising; since then, channels for advertising have grown exponentially. As our attention spans dwindle and we consume more information, business owners often find themselves overwhelmed by the number of advertising options. To get their brand in front of your face, business owners need to guess where their potential customers will get the advertising message. And advertising sales people are happy to label their solutions to this problem as "the one."

Lessons Learned: Don't Hire the Ad Rep. Hire the Ad

It doesn't matter how charming the advertising sales rep is. If you don't believe that you, as a buyer, would be compelled to act on an ad for services like yours through the medium the advertiser is trying to sell, walk away.

Consider your advertising dollars to be like a stock investment. You want a positive return on your advertisements. If that is not likely with a given advertising medium, invest your advertising dollars somewhere else.

Put That Away

I remember when I brought a Yellow Pages sales guy into my house/business and welcomed him to my kitchen table/office. He explained the options available, and I picked a few I thought would bring a return. After I signed a contract and gave him a check, he pulled out a big piece of paper and started scribbling an ad together. Keep in mind that I have a graphic design background, so I am fairly confident in my knowledge and skill in design. I grew less than confident in his. But apparently, this is just standard practice for many advertisers. They want your money now. The idea that you would pay them routinely if the ads were successful because of, for example, great design, seemed to have escaped most advertisers' notice. I was dumbfounded. But hey, maybe this guy happens to be a designer, right? I mean, I was fixing printers at the time and had a design background, which was atypical. I gave the guy the benefit of the doubt. Poor decision. I was suddenly put in a place of having to tell someone to whom I just gave money that their design was terrible. It was worthless. From this experience, I realized that I had to design my own ad. Which meant investing more time.

Lessons Learned: Advertising Costs Money or Time... or Both

I committed to spending the money on a Yellow Pages ad, and I committed to designing the ad. For me, these investments were a commitment to bringing in some business. I had no intention of paying money just to watch it go away. I was expecting a handsome return.

You need to treat advertising like this. Maybe your business will thrive with minimal awareness alone. But in my case, I believed that people would flip through the Yellow Pages looking for a printer repair company, find me, and dial me. In the meantime, the advertising salesperson was only hoping my check would cash.

I continued to learn valuable lessons in business from advertising salespeople. I tried out text ads a few years later. It was an expensive option, but it was new and exciting and promised rainbows and moonbeams of success. So I bit. It was a dismal failure. It was so brutally unsuccessful that I wondered if anyone had even seen the message until a few spam leads popped up in response to the ads. At least we know someone saw them.

Another lesson came when I was asked to sign up for a text marketing campaign again by the same salesperson. I couldn't believe what I was hearing. On one hand, I understood the request. Maybe he didn't notice it was a dismal failure and hoped I'd continue to pay. On quite the other (and arguably more ethical) hand, how could someone sell something that failed so miserably and have the gall to ask for another sale?

> **"The only people who care about advertising are the people who work in advertising."**
>
> -George Parker

Oh What a Feeling

Your business may or may not be boring, but to truly market it well, you must advertise the feeling your customers will get after their experience with you.

Do beer companies typically use their ads to describe the flavor of their product? Nope. They're showing straight-up freezing cold temperatures, a train plowing dangerously close to the biggest party on this side of your 21st birthday, girls in bikinis, people laughing and dancing, whistles blowing... and beer just happens to be there. No one seems to be getting frostbite, despite the arctic setting. Beer companies sell the beer by marketing the party. You're giving your potential consumers a glimpse at the feelings they'll (hopefully) get from your product or service.

The odd yet beautiful thing about marketing is that consumers are rarely surprised when they purchase a product but don't get the results that were essentially promised.

> **"In our factory, we make lipstick. In our advertising, we sell hope."**
>
> -Charles Revson, co-founder of Revlon

For example, when you shampoo your hair, do you have an orgasm? When you bite into a chip, does a talking Cheetah show up to make your life more enjoyable? Does celebrity endorsement make you feel like you're ready to sign a multi-million-dollar sports contract when you run in those shoes?

The answer to these questions is probably no, even though it's exactly what the advertising suggested. So why don't we get upset when the fantasies don't come true? Furthermore, why do we continue to buy products after consistently broken promises? The answer is simply, "Who cares?" Use the psychology of influence to your advantage in business. Look for the hope, the sensations, and the awesomeness that your product has even the remotest chance of inducing.

Lessons Learned: The Ad Needs to Sell What the Consumer Wants to Buy

Most ads should trigger an emotion. For example, you aren't buying cough syrup, you are buying a remedy to your illness so you can get your work done without grossing out your clients.

Essentially, you should illustrate what your customer will experience when they purchase and use your product or service. Spray yourself with Axe and watch the girls pile on you. Vote for that candidate or watch the world crumble into an apocalyptic pile of garbage. You can use marketing to define the experience and culture of your product or service as well as your brand.

> *"Many a large thing has been made large by the right kind of advertising."*
> -Mark Twain

Buy Me Buy Me Buy Me

In advertising, your brand essentially needs to answer two key questions: "What do you do?" and "Who do you do it for?" If you can throw in an answer to the question, "Why should the customer choose you?" all the better. Importantly, your business will not be asked questions like this, even figuratively, if you are not marketing your business. That is to say, if no one knows your business exists, how would they know to ask you questions about it?

Consumers are inundated with advertisements all over the place, all the time. They are bombarded with communications and content that have little to no value beyond advertising. Your job is to be noticed among the millions of bits of information that your target market sees, hears, and experiences every day. This can be tough to do.

Lessons Learned: Advertising is Expensive

I had dreams of grandeur for my business when I first started it: TV and radio ads galore to scream to the masses that I was here and ready to serve. Then I saw a few price lists for broadcast advertising. It gave me new insight into the cost of business.

Influence

Let's look at a few other aspects of getting people to buy your product or service. Robert Cialdini, in his highly acclaimed book, *Influence: The Psychology of Persuasion*, detailed six principles of influence. They are reciprocation, social proof, consistency, trust, authority, and scarcity. Let's dive into each to find out where it fits into your business.

> "*Our best evidence of what people truly feel and believe comes less from their words than from their deeds.*"
> -Robert Cialdini

Principle 1: Reciprocation is almost automatic for most people. When you do something for me, I feel obligated to do something for you, even if the thing you did for me was something I didn't want or ask for. You can give potential clients free samples, information, or some other unexpected free gift. You know all of those return address labels you receive from non-profits? That is

153

reciprocity in motion.

Principle 2: Social proof is evident far beyond your real-world network. These days, it extends into the digital realm as well. See all those reviews on Amazon from people you don't even know? How many followers does a person have? How many views did a video get? We trust what the crowds do, and we're often not even aware of it. Have you ever seen a crowd outside a cell phone store for the newest iPhone? This still blows my mind, though I see it working all the time. Have you ever decided on a purchase based on testimonials from people you have never met? As a marketer, all you need to show is that others are doing it, which tells your potential customers that they should too.

Principle 3: Consistency is simple and powerful. It uses the idea that people want to be who they believe they are. If you get someone to agree to do something before it's time to do it, they'll want to maintain consistency and go along with what they said they'd do. The art and science of this combine when you find the exact timing of when to ask and when to deliver. For example, if you get someone to tell you they work out routinely right before you offer to sell them a treadmill, they will be more compelled to buy.

Principle 4: Trust should be a no-brainer. People buy from people they like and trust. People like and trust those who are most like themselves. Generally speaking, if you are nice to me, look good, show up on time, and follow through, I'll probably be more inclined to buy from you. Introduce matching breathing and speaking patterns to me and I will feel like we are long lost cousins.

Principle 5: Authority is all about respect. People who demonstrate confidence and intelligence come across as being great to buy from. Even job titles lend authority that encourages people to buy. Perhaps that's why almost every banker is a vice president of something. This is also why some marketers bring in famous people to hawk their wares. Irrelevance doesn't matter—authority is authority to many potential customers. That's why

Michael Jordan sells underwear.

Principle 6: Scarcity is hard to come by. Not really, but it was fun to imagine, right? Scarcity is using the tactic of getting the potential client to believe that they have a limited time to act or the product goes away. Countdowns often get people to buy now. Ebay built an empire on this over a few years. Online stores warn you that there are only "3 left," and so on.

> "*Advertising is the 'wonder' in Wonder Bread.*"
>
> -Jef I. Richards

Couldn't some of these principles be used to sell people things they don't need? Absolutely. In fact, they're likely to have been used this way. That said, some people aren't sure what they want, and as a bold business owner, you're probably selling something worth having. Giving a potential client a little kick using these principles rather than relying on other disorderly methods may prove to be a blessing to you and your clients.

Another thing to be aware of is that you too are being sold to, even by your clients. They want a discount or free service or sample products or some other deal to help them on their journey. This is all part of the marketing, advertising, and negotiating game. Consider this knowledge one more tool in your marketing belt.

Lessons Learned: Principles vs. Profit

When I attended sales training, some expressed apprehension at learning some forbidden secret that, they felt, could be used for evil. To me, this seemed like an excuse to avoid learning effective sales and communication. Like learning a martial art, it certainly could be used to harm others. The point is that you will be better for knowing these skills and that you'll be able to use them to save yourself from being a victim of them. The fact that you will improve your clients' lives by encouraging them to purchase while navigating their natural apprehension to being sold to is how this knowledge will shine.

Selling You on Sales

Everybody is in sales. Even if you're a one-person company selling your services to one other company (not a recommended business practice), you are in sales. When you want a vendor to give you a discount, a client to back down, or even the delivery person to go the extra distance, you're making a sale. Any and all skills, experience, and time in the sales trenches will help you now and in the future. You can never be too good of a salesperson.

Now take your mad sales skills and apply them to your marketing. Looking at all that you put out into the world, would you buy from you? If the answer is no, then change what you're saying or how or where you're saying it.

Should I Advertise Here

I received an email from a coaching client of mine the other day. He had a question typical of a new and growing small business. The message went like this:

> Dear James,
> I got a cold call today from someadcompany.com about buying a print ad in their magazine. They make Playbill-sized magazines for four golf clubs in town, including this fancy club and that other fancy club. They claim they only put two to three companies in each category in the magazine. It's $600 for a half-page ad.
> I never thought about using print advertising, but this magazine is targeted at active/athletic people with money. Is it worth buying an ad as an experiment? What are your thoughts?
> Sincerely,
> Awesome Client

I replied in glorious detail. Keep in mind that the response shared below was written for a client with a very specific clientele (athletes with injuries). However, the reasoning stands for any advertising you may consider with your own business.

Dear Awesome Client,
I've decided to tackle your question from a few angles to make sure you are well informed. Hopefully you can use it to navigate the shark-filled waters of paid advertising:

Money.
To justify paying for a $600 ad, how many paid appointments do you need to get? My rough calculations say that based on your rates and profit margin, you will need 50 appointments (from current $12 gross profit from each appointment) from this ad. Is this ad likely to bring that in?
Of course, you may get a few clients that will return monthly, so there may be a return that isn't immediate. How many sessions will one typical routine client sign up for? If the answer is ten or more, you need only five new clients.

Brand.
Maybe the money doesn't shake out, but the whole brand recognition thing is a possibility, right? A golfer sees the ad, thinks of her broken friend, and sends him to you. Or someone sees another ad of yours somewhere else and connects the dots, leading to brand recognition. But this is a stretch. Unless you have thousands of dollars to spend on advertising, you're banking on your potential clients being in the right place at the right time routinely enough to recognize, remember, and therefore use or refer you. Are you advertising through enough combined mediums that brand recognition is a possibility?
Options.

$600 will get you a lot of targeted ads on Google, Facebook, and other online options. You could pound one of these for that same $600 and reach thousands of people who are explicitly looking for what you offer. Digital options allow you to see the end results and the actions of users who saw or interacted with the ads. Can the golf magazine offer that? Nothing in print can. Until they offer clickable paper or remote eye movement scans, this is a limitation that must be reflected in the price and the measured value of print advertising.

You could also letter up the back half of your car for $600. How many people see the tail end of your cruiser every day?

Alternatively, you could do an Every Door Direct Mail campaign and reach hundreds of people multiple times in the areas where these golfers live.

You may even choose to pay a high-school kid $10/hour for a solid 40-hour week of door-knocking with money left over for commission.

You could offer referral bonuses to existing clients.

You could pay yourself to prospect your existing contacts.

Reality.

Let's pretend you're a golfer. You show up, rent a cart, and hit the holes. You page through this Playbill thing while waiting for your buddy to figure out how to find a golf ball in an obnoxiously thick marsh. Let's also pretend that there's a coupon in there for "Free Hugs and a Million Dollars" from a cute drink-cart girl. How many people will see, decide, and act on that ad? Is it 50?

How does your offer compare to free hugs and a million dollars?

I hate telling people to not advertise, but in this case and in my opinion, your money is better spent elsewhere.

Sincerely,

James

So how do you figure out where to advertise? Here's where a bit of easy math comes in. First, we have to lay down some assumptions, some that can be tweaked to fit your business. We need to know or assume that:

1. **You can afford to advertise.** If you cannot, start knocking on doors and calling on potential customers until you can afford to advertise.

2. **You know what your maximum capacity is.** Let us just assume that the advertising works. Let's assume it works crazy well—it was just featured on the Google homepage for a week and endorsed by Oprah. Suddenly, you have a burst of clients and purchases and, therefore, problems. You want to be able to know when to start closing the spigot.

3. **You know, roughly, what percentage of each sale is profit** (profit, as in ready-to-be-put-in-your-personal-bank-account profit). Since assuming the break-even point means that the monthly bills (rent, employees, taxes, etc.) are paid for, you only have to worry about the direct costs associated with each additional sale. If you don't know this number, I recommend you figure it out. If a client doesn't know the number, even a rough idea, I often guess about 40%. (So for every $100 you bring in after your break-even point, assume you'll pocket $40. The other $60 will pay for the product, service, employees, upkeep, or extra costs that come with additional sales.) Assuming 40% doesn't work well with software- or other intellectual property-type items, but it works like magic for most services.

4. **You know the cost of the advertisement.** This should be a simple bit of information to gather; however, you may be surprised at how many people set up ads (especially online ads) and watch the monthly expenses run away from their ideal target. A $20 daily-budget for online ads seems like a nice amount until

the end of the month rolls around and you see a $600 bill with only a few email addresses to show for it.

5.   **You know what to expect.** Advertising is like shooting a machine gun at a large room full of hundreds of zombies. If you can only afford one bullet and it takes three bullets to kill one zombie, you're going to have a bad day, go broke, and end up eating brains. If you can afford three bullets, you better be a damn good shot and a fast runner. If you can afford 3000 bullets, well now you're almost enjoying the process. The zombies will get sick of seeing you and may just buy from you as they follow the crowd.

6.   **Leave your hopes of brand recognition at the door** unless you plan to spend more than $3000. Think of Coca-Cola or Budweiser. If they spent your advertising budget in the local area you serve, would they be popular? Can you imagine only seeing one beer ad of any kind in a month? You know these brands because they pound and pound until your head hurts. Then they pound some more. And they invest millions of dollars in that pounding. In 2014 alone, Budweiser spent over $108 million dollars on advertising. That's just one brand of beer. Coca-Cola had an advertising budget of over $3.9 billion for 2015. (And that's billion, with a b.) You, on the other hand, probably need to be a bit more frugal. At least, for now.

7.   **You know the medium will actually reach people.** I still receive a few Yellow Pages books on my doorstep. They get smaller every year, but they still show up. Last year, I received a card that stated, "If you would like a real book, let us know." Can you imagine paying to be in a book that isn't even actively distributed? Some people are still paying to advertise in certain mediums either because they don't know any better or because that's where their business is coming

from. If these places will work for you, great. If not, find another place or just save your money.

8.   **You are aware of your options.** The client email I shared earlier was in response to a cold call. My client was about to lay down $600 from one cold call. Who says cold calling is dead? Instead of purchasing the ad, my client could have paid $600 for someone to make cold calls on his behalf or he could pay himself to make those calls. If he were ready to buy in response to a cold call, why wouldn't someone else be?

Choices, Options and Selections

The options for advertising are essentially endless: radio, TV, internet, vehicles, buses, newspapers, and uniforms of race-car drivers. Can you look up from this book now and not see an ad? You have choices, including the option not to advertise.

What I'm hoping to convey is that advertising is expensive, though it can be worth it. Remember that $3.9 billion Coca-Cola paid in 2015 for advertising? They had sales of over $44 billion in that same year. Keep in mind that they are essentially selling sugar water. So perhaps their profit margin is a little higher than yours. Imagine if Coca-Cola only spent $30,000 annually on advertising. Would they be the brand people know today?

You should also ask yourself whether you really need your brand to be a "brand." If you can get away with being a local brand, you have a much better chance of being known. Be aware that oftentimes the appeal of universal brand recognition is rooted in a business owner's ego. I'm not saying not to go for brand recognition. There is a time and place for brand recognition, but there is also a cost. That cost is tough to recoup in the small business arena.

Think of it like this, Coca-Cola needs every person over the age of 12 to know they exist. What is your demographic? Is it that diverse? Or does it lean more towards that of my client? His target demographic is active men and women aged 18-59 who weigh less than 200 pounds and do more than 20 hours per week of physical activity. He could spend millions on advertising and not get a great return because there's a limit to who needs to know about him. He has a max capacity of 53 client sessions a month, so he only needs 53 people to show up and pay him every month. Based on the average 2% response rate for some advertising, he only needs his ads to hit 2700 people that are his target client. He needs those people to be hit with those ads multiple times. If he found an advertising medium to hit his target demographic of 2700 people multiple times, he would be booked solid in a relatively short time. With the current frequency of repeat clients and resulting referrals he could add employees and continue to grow. Could a golf book do that?

It's more likely that your business also has to pay you for time beyond the time you actually spend providing your service: time for work on picking out where or if to advertise, time running invoices and billing, time to meet with your accountant, time to network, time to deal with employees or subcontractors. All of the time you work but are not directly getting paid needs to be reimbursed. This is a must for you to survive.

Bright Screens

We live in a world now where lighters are no longer held up at concerts. Phones are held up with animated gifs of flames instead. As a practical issue, this is much better than the previous fire hazard of 10,000 lighters being held up by a drunk crowd. It is interesting to note that we value communication so much that we bring our main communication devices with us even to concerts we have paid hundreds of dollars to attend.

That also means that just about everybody can see one of your ads on their little technologically advanced addiction.

Is All This Really Necessary

Behind all this is the challenge of deciding if you should advertise, and if so, where and how often? These are difficult questions that no one has a solid answer to. Just as no one can predict the stock market with 100% accuracy, no one can predict which advertising will work best for your business. Add in the constantly changing advertising landscape, popular mediums coming and going, and it starts to feel like quite the moving target. In any case, there are still some basic steps that you can take to make a decision that you can feel confident in.

> *"Half the money I spend on advertising is wasted; the trouble is I don't know which half."*
> -John Wanamaker

First, you need to determine how many of your ideal clients you need to get in front of. How? Figure out how many units you want to sell and how much you can make on each unit. Next determine how many people need to know you exist in order to sell that number of units.

For example, if you need to sell 100 units per month and 2% of the ideal clients that see your advertisement purchase from you, you know you need to get in front of 5000 ideal clients per month. You must also consider the initial capital outlay and the resulting delay between the marketing message and the actual purchase of your product.

This can be determined by understanding your customer's past buying behavior. Also being aware that some products are fast movers and some are slow. Think a pizza ad during the Superbowl vs. a billboard for an injury lawyer on the highway. Essentially it is a best guess, just as with choosing the advertising medium itself.

Then you need to determine your budget. Typical budget guidelines range from 5-7% of your sales as a standard or 20-30% of your entire annual budget if you are just starting.

Think of your budget like a container of water. If you take that water and splash it on as many people as possible, most won't realize you exist. If you take that water and douse a few targeted people, they will certainly know you exist. You need to match your budget to the volume of people you need to reach.

We'd like to believe that the more we spend on advertising, the more we will gain in revenue. Something like this:

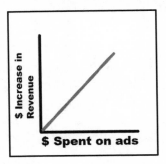

In reality, it takes a bigger chunk of money to prime the advertising pump to actually get a return to spout. At some point, your dollars spent on advertising will lead to a predictable return on your investment. Then those returns will begin to level off. So advertising looks more like this:

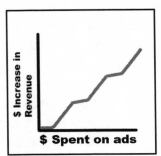

The challenge is finding the initial point when your advertising actually nets a return. Then keep pumping that advertising well. The point when advertising levels off most businesses do not need to worry about.

Check Me Out

After all of that, you need to decide on where you will

advertise. Will you take a focused approach and use pay-per-click or a social media site that uses data to show the right ad to the right person? Or will you use a broadcast medium such as TV or radio that may have tens of thousands of people in their audience? Ultimately, the challenge is determining which medium works best for your business.

Generally speaking, if your ideal clients make up less than 10% of the population, you should go for focused ads, typically online. If your target audience makes up more than 10% of the population, it may make sense to consider broadcast mediums whose viewers, listeners, or readers strongly represent the demographics of your ideal client.

When determining the volume of your ideal clients in a given population, consider where the advertising mediums reach. Websites can reach globally or locally; radio stations can reach for dozens of miles. An example would be a small cafe on the far east side of a large town. Though TV, radio, and newspaper may reach a great portion of the population, only a small portion of the population would consider going due to location alone. So perhaps those aren't ideal options. Something more targeted like direct mail or geographic based web ads would be better. A car dealership, on the other hand, may love TV, radio, and newspaper since their ideal clients are part of a broader audience and are often willing to travel farther to make a purchase.

> "Good advertising does not just circulate information. It penetrates the public mind with desires and belief."
> -Leo Burnett

Weeee!

The best part about advertising is that it's fun. It's enjoyable to create the ads and discover what works. For my first business, we had a live copier-smashing event in the style of Office Space, the movie, at the end of a local baseball game. One of the actors, Richard Riehle, was a guest at the baseball game signing autographs. We tied in with his presence to promote the event. The entire infield was filled with copiers and printers being destroyed by a semi-inebriated crowd. It was an awesome event that quickly turned into a challenge—it turns out that after a few beers and if given a bat, people will not wait in line to smash a copier. Who knew? It was a little glimpse of what anarchy would look like. Luckily, it did connect my company's brand with office machines and fun, which was the purpose. Years later, we still laugh at that event. As we were cleaning up the millions of bits of office machine from the baseball diamond, the manager said, "That was fun. We will never do it again."

Chapter 10

Sales are something you should buy into.

6 6

"Record sales don't really mean anything. For us,
the pressure is imagining some 15-year-old kid in
Cincinnati who buys our album and doesn't feel
like he wasted his pocket money."

9 9   -Chris Martin (Lead singer for Coldplay)

Sales is one of those words that scare people. Businesses need sales, yet most business owners hate to sell. That puts you, as a business owner, in a pickle. Do you become all that you hate in the world and sell your product or service by pitching it to everyone you meet? Or do you sit idly by the phone and wait for the orders to show up based on sheer hope? My suggestion is to find a mix that suits you even if it brings you outside of your comfort zone. Your business will not sell itself, and dust on your products cannot be traded in for cash.

If you are OK banging phones and schmoozing with the

best sales people, you can almost be guaranteed to be successful. Why? Because sales, as a profession, is booming and it works. Salespeople are needed in this world. Understand that if you are a great salesperson, it will make owning a business much easier.

We are all just squirrels trying to get a nut. This chapter will deal with some of the dos and don'ts in regard to sales. You really only need one "do." Sell. Period. Get out there and talk to people. Pick up the phone, jump on your email, bark at passers-by. Whatever you need to do, just sell. Your business is literally nothing without customers. Those customers need to buy. In order for those customers to buy, they need to be sold to. You need to start that process.

◢ Lessons Learned: Sell, Sell, Sell

Sales is a skill that can be learned. Take the time to learn how to sell. Before you do that, though, try to sell on your own and grow a few extra layers of skin. You will need them to deal with the lying, back-stabbing people that you try to sell to. People will generally have some loathing for salespeople since most people have bought something they regretted. Are you selling something people will regret buying? Probably not, so you have no reason not to sell. Go do it. Now!

Sales Dos and Don'ts: Politics and Religion and Oh Boy...

I have a rule for my employees when they speak with anyone while they're in a business setting: Do not talk about religion or politics. No good can come from it. I believe sports, TV, and weather are popular topics because many people want to avoid talking about religion and politics.

The reason behind my advice is that you don't want to disagree with a client and lose business over an issue that has nothing to do with your business. For example, if you are for or against immigration reform, would you want to discuss this with your mechanic? First of all, if you disagree with your mechanic's stance, I would double check the bolts on your car. The repair bill may also be a little padded. People will do crazy things over polarizing issues. If people are willing to light themselves on fire, send planes into buildings, or murder doctors, they will have no problem avoiding doing business with you or another company. Note that another company may disagree with your client as well. This particular zealot just happens not to know that, which makes it a non-issue and leads to more cash in the neutral company's pocket. Money is pretty cool, so you want to maintain your neutrality.

When I told my friends about this rule, they challenged me. (That's why they're my friends.) At the time, the big news was what bathrooms transgender people should be allowed to use. People were preparing to "guard" bathrooms against people going into what they believed was the wrong door. Religion was getting involved, the president got involved, and newspapers everywhere had something to write about it.

Target had just announced that you can pee where you believe you were meant to pee, provided it is in a restroom and specifically in a toilet of some kind. Immediately, some people got excited and started protesting Target. Target's stock dropped almost 30% within a couple of weeks. My friends asked why Target would take a stance like this if not talking about religion or politics was a sound business rule.

My answer included a few points. First, Target is a big company; they are big enough to get into issues like this on occasion. Does Target take a daily stance on every new issue? Nope. They got into the fray because Target has the public going into its stores, and every once in awhile, the public has to pee. Target saw an opportunity to protect its brand by tarnishing it a little bit. This is one of those "if you want to make an omelet, you need to break some eggs" cases. Religious and political people get momentarily excited, then they lose their fervor and go back to the store. Any store. The most convenient store that makes them feel good. That might be their local Target.

Maybe it stopped people from using the bathrooms at Target, which, from my experience, is a good thing when you're the person who has to clean it.

Target was the first major company to take a stance on this issue, so they received a ton of publicity. For free. Have you ever been to a Target store? You are more than likely aware of Target for three reasons: 1) publicity, 2) marketing, and 3) a huge building that holds all of the essential items you need, plus some. Numbers 2 and 3 above cost money, but Number 1 is fairly cheap. All you need to do is stick your neck out a little bit. This was a hot-button issue at the time, and Target gained some brand recognition while making the transgender community feel more welcome. By making the transgender community feel more welcome, they made other people feel more welcome. They sent out a message that said, "Target cares about you as a society." They took a stance against hate to make a statement as well as reinforce their brand.

The important detail is what political or religious issue Target, or any business, chooses to stick their neck out for. Can you imagine Target taking on a bigger political issue and continually reinforcing it? How many companies do you know made campaign contributions? Most large companies do. Do they put up a billboard telling the world how much they gave to what politician and what they are hoping to accomplish from that investment?

"We gave $5 million to the whatever party in hopes of them easing

restrictions on this and that so that we can net a profit of $250 million from this contribution."

Not a news story you will likely see.

> **"I'm tired of hearing about money, money, money, money, money. I just want to play the game, drink Pepsi, wear Reebok."**
>
> -Shaquille O'Neal

In any case, this bold business book is not geared at companies that large. What should a small business do? Talk about the weather. Or the client's families or hobbies, or perhaps discuss the fun of what the people are paying you to do. Get to know the person you're speaking with. They may be much more interesting than any weather, sports, or politics. Whatever you do, avoid religion and politics like the plague. The challenge is how to react when a client says something like, "Can you believe what so-and-so said during that debate? What an idiot!"

It doesn't matter if you agree or not. The goal is to steer the conversation to neutral. Let me give you an example of how you might do this. I don't watch sports. For me to sit in one place for three hours and call it entertainment is not likely to happen. Many people do, and that's just fine with me. I can shop at Target during a football game and actually get through the store quickly. But one day, I ended up at a party chatting with one of my wife's colleagues and the talk turned to sports.

Guy at Party: Can you believe that pass in the 4th quarter?

Me: I know, right? Who has hands like that?

Guy at Party: Isn't it crazy what the refs did to <insert famous sports name here that I don't recognize and cannot pronounce>?

171

Me: That is crazy. How did you like their defense?

Guy at Party: It was awesome! The way <other famous sports name here that I don't recognize and cannot pronounce> blocked the blah, blah, blah.

Me: That was impressive. But the offense is what really surprised me. Do you think they can get better?

Guy at Party: Blah, blah, blah...

This went on until my wife came over and ruined the charade by exclaiming, "You don't even watch sports!" (Mental note: If I ever need to commit a crime, I cannot tell my wife.)

The way to keep the conversation neutral is to keep asking vague questions. You can control the conversation and contribute nothing to it, and the other person in the conversation is likely to have no idea that you weren't contributing. Questions like, "Do you think they can get any better?" could be interpreted as meaning that either they are poor now and need to get better or they are great now and they could get better. It's a question that relies on the interpretation of your conversational partner.

The art of good business is controlling the conversation without the other person knowing. If someone says something like, "Can you believe the viewpoint I have on this ultra-controversial issue?" you can reply with something like, "It's interesting that this is being brought to light now, isn't it?" You did not agree. You did not disagree. You continued the conversation. Eventually, you can move the conversation to anything you want through diversion tactics such as dropping your pen and moving the topic to options for ink colors or (preferably) ask a question that changes the focus of your conversational partner. It goes like this:

Ultra-controversial conversationalist: The people have spoken, and they want not only X, but Y and Z as well. And we are going to get it.

You: I never noticed that you had a picture of a sticky kid on your desk. How old is that walking jar of jelly now?

Controlling conversations is a powerful tool in business. Being aware when someone else is controlling the conversation is also a great tool. It works in negotiations and sales as well as conversations you need to have with employees and managers. It also works with vendors and, dare I say, your spouse and kids. Apply these rules to actions rather than words, and you can train your pets with this tool.

 Lessons Learned: Humans are Social Creatures

Humans are social creatures. We thrive on interaction. Sure, we want to be alone every once in awhile. Some people are certainly just too annoying to persuade us to hang out with them. But selling is a social game. You have to have a conversation with someone to sell them something. It should be fun. At least a little.

Sales Dos and Don'ts: And vs. But in Your Conversations

In many of my conversations (and even in writing this book) I've caught myself messing up this simple rule. If you are making a point that switches gears with a "but," your conversation sounds like, "This is a big deal and this is a big deal, but I am not addressing those facts or taking them into account now to support my argument." However, if you change "but" to "and," your conversation comes off as more authentic and as if you are taking all facts into account. For example, you will sound like this, "This is a big deal and this is a big deal, and I am addressing those facts as well as taking them into account now to support my argument."

Sales Dos and Don'ts: Treat the Prospect Like a Human

Everybody deserves respect and a chance to buy what you are selling. Your job is to sell to people in order to get them to buy so both you and the customer are happy. You are not above or below them. You are equals.

173

> *"Pretend that every single person you meet has a sign around his or her neck that says, 'Make me feel important.' Not only will you succeed in sales, you will succeed in life."*
> -Mary Kay Ash

Sales Dos and Don'ts: Accept the No

When you ask anyone a question, you are expecting an answer. That answer in sales is often "no." In fact, the hardest part about selling for many people can be attributed to dealing with the "no." They feel like the prospect is turning them down personally. I may love you, but it is unlikely that I am going to buy a vacuum cleaner from you. No is just a way for you to verify that this prospect will not be purchasing from you. It may be a no forever, a no for now, or a no in the form of "Yes, but I have no money." It really doesn't matter. What matters is that you ask. As many people as you can, as best you can. The yes responses will come if you ask enough.

> *"Never take no from somebody who cannot say yes."*
> -Adam Braun

Sales Dos and Don'ts: What Not to Say

How many times do you get the idea that you know more than the person you're talking with because they say something like, "Ummmmm…" when asked a simple question such as "How many slices of toast can this toaster toast?" It is pretty easy, right? They don't seem to know anything. Or nothing in regard to what you're asking. How do you appear to someone when you say these phrases:

"Ummmmm."

"You know…"

Sales are something you should buy into

"Like…"

"Not a problem."

"Yep."

In the flow of conversation, some of these may make sense. Do you, like, know what I mean? Yep. Not a problem.

> **"Precise language is not the problem. Clear language is the problem."**
> -Richard P. Feynman

Sales Dos and Don'ts: When in Doubt, Fill Your Pipeline

As your business grows you will find yourself with some nice downtime. Employees and vendors are working hard for you, money is flowing and life is grand. When you have those moments, be sure to continue to keep your sales pipeline full. Get in front of people and have some fun with it.

Sales are the foundation of your business. Without sales you have a very expensive hobby. Pick up the phone, send an email, write a letter (remember those?) or add some content to your website. Keep doing something daily to add volume to your pipeline. Even when things are going well. Especially when things are going well.

> **"What you do today can improve all your tomorrows."**
> -Ralph Marston

Money Matters

I just got off the phone with a business friend of mine. He's a smart person who decided to get into the small business world. After speaking with him for a few minutes, I realized his problem is his skewed perception of the value of a dollar. Because of this, he doesn't charge what he should. For little jobs, he often doesn't charge at all. The worst part is that these "little jobs" constitute nearly half of the work he does.

He believes that money is tight for just about everyone. Because of this belief, he wants to save the world by devaluing his own products and services. He will not end world hunger and you probably won't either. Or, at least, not by reducing your prices. The people who buy from you probably buy because they see value in what you offer. If you don't value your own products and services, why should anyone else?

The challenge for many people, myself included, is how do you price your products and service? You need to price yourself at a point above where you think your price should be. How many times do you find out what competitors charge and you are floored that they can charge that? Learn from that. What are they doing that builds perceived value to their clients? Can you do something that will build more value with your clients?

If your clients see the value, they will pay what you ask. If they do not, they won't. You need to feel uncomfortable with what you charge. That will make up for at least some of the head trash you have that tells you that you aren't worth it. You are worth it. Compact your head trash and make room for giving your clients all that you can.

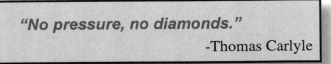

> **"No pressure, no diamonds."**
> -Thomas Carlyle

I grew up in a house where money was tight. I assumed that my parents were chasing some elusive dollars and that those dollars were awfully fast. It took me decades to realize that their quest for money was spent chasing it away the more they tried to reach it. A small business owner client had this same mentality. Because of his perception that cash has a lower value than many people believe it does, he was also complaining of the cost of things he was being offered. Some things that he even bought. He complained of how expensive things like insurance, training, and generally most products and services are. He felt he was overcharged for nearly everything. So his pricing model reflected what he thought the value of a dollar was. If everything is expensive in your mind except for your prices, perhaps the value of a dollar in your mind is out of sync.

The personal perception of the value of a dollar can make or break a company, or a lifestyle for that matter. If you can spend $1000 and earn $20,000 as a result, will you complain about spending the initial $1000? You would be surprised how many people will. I used to be one of them. My point is that things often cost more than we believe they should. After we spend the money on these things, we either realize they were worth it, realize we got screwed, or we forget the purchase altogether and move along with our lives.

If you want a very interesting read on the psychology of pricing, check out the book *Priceless* by William Poundstone. It will frighten you how easily swayed a mind can be in regards to numbers and pricing.

> "*You miss 100% of the shots you don't take.*"
> -Wayne Gretzky

Negotiation

There have been countless books written on negotiation, so I'll save the deep delving into that topic for other authors. For this BOLD book, let me offer this advice: Everything is negotiable, and, generally speaking, if you are nice and look good you'll get further in your negotiations.

The gift of gab cannot be underestimated. Through all of your networking with others in business and industry, you will gain knowledge and skill in communication that will help you with negotiations better than most books ever can. Seeing a master negotiator in action is powerful and fun. Sometimes I even get suckered on purpose just to watch a great salesperson work her sales game. At least I like to think it's on purpose. Education is rarely free but always worth it.

My advice, if you're not the best at negotiating, is to try some baby steps. Ask for something special or rare at the next restaurant or hotel you visit. Maybe ask for an extra bag at the grocery store. Regardless of what the request is, the first step is to get into the mindset of asking and watching the reaction of the person you are asking. Ask if you can have two samples from the lady offering samples of sausage at the grocery store. These are little steps that will blossom into powerful skills.

The art of negotiation is to either get something for nothing or something for much less than your perceived value of it. The trick is to get the other party to either want to give you that something for free or severely discounted or to believe that they were the winner in the negotiation. Winning at negotiation is all about perception. It's not unusual at all for a negotiation to end with each negotiator thinking they won. The art of compromise comes down to your communication.

For example, suppose you put a desk for sale on Craigslist. You put a price of $100 for the thing because it retails for over $700. It's not that old, but it happens to be blocking your path since you replaced it. You want it out of your way more than you want a 100% cash return. You place the ad with your cell number and wait for someone to respond. In a day or so, you receive a text that says only, "Take $50 for the desk." Do you accept that offer? It seems like it's either from a kid that doesn't have $50 or a serial killer, neither of which will do you much good at getting rid of the desk.

If, instead, you receive a call about the ad and the caller starts asking questions about the desk, that caller can accomplish a few things. First, they can gain some rapport with you. Next, they can find and point out flaws in your pricing algorithm. Then, they can weigh the pain of you having to deal with creepy text people or having this desk in your way until it's sold. And finally, they can make the move to let you know that this pain can be relieved today and that they will give you $50. In less than four minutes, you sold your desk and the buyer "saved" 50%. This may be a negotiation in which both of you come away thinking you won. But who really won? Both of you.

This is also a reason why some people are afraid of answering their phone. They may be worried that they will be suckered into agreeing to do, sell, or buy something that they wouldn't have if they had been given time to think. If you sincerely feel this way, get out in the real world a bit more. If you believe that you cannot be suckered over text or email, I have a rich uncle from Nigeria that recently passed away. He has $500,000 in savings that he would like to share with you if you will just help his nephew get it into the US.

> "I never go looking for a sucker.
> I look for a champion and make a
> sucker out of him."
> -Amarillo Slim

If It Ain't Yes, What is It?

I have a rule in my sales process. At the end of every encounter with a prospect I get a yes, no, or a clear next step. A yes is great, as you can imagine. A no is fine too; I can move along to greener pastures. I do not accept wishy-washy terms such as "let me think it over" or "email me something." You need the prospect to commit to a clear next step. Otherwise, you're left guessing what the prospect actually has in mind. And I'm guessing you are about as great at reading minds as I am. (I am not that great at reading minds.)

It goes like this. "Hey, prospecty-person, I know you're not ready to make a decision now. Would it make sense for me to call you next Tuesday afternoon to check in and see if we can move forward? If this is not a good fit, I want you to feel free to tell me so I don't waste any of your time." You are detailing how and when you will contact the prospect and giving them an easy out by literally asking them to tell you no. This is often a great place to get any objections or questions laid out. You can simply ask, "What will you need to see for us to move ahead with this on Tuesday?"

Lessons Learned: Ask for the Sale

This is just one of those things that seems so silly to me, mainly because I still am guilty of it too. You get a conversation going, you're laughing and having a great time, but you never actually ask for the sale. Or you never get to prospecting. Get out and talk to people. Ask them to buy from you.

Sales is just like volleyball or tennis. You score when the ball is in the other person's court. All you need to do is return the ball. You return the ball by asking questions.

Why You Need to Give Away the Store
by Spencer Smith, Spencer X Smith Consulting
spencerxsmith.com

A famous book publisher approaches you with an offer. This publisher has helped make the careers of people you admire and would love to emulate.

She tells you, "I've been following your personal brand and need to publish your story. Will you please give me your very best ideas to share with the world?"

Would you do it? Of course!

Can you think of any negatives to this situation? Is there any reason why you wouldn't do it?

Let me explain:

Here are the two concerns I hear after I tell people they should share their expertise via digital and social media:

If I give away my best ideas for free, why would anyone pay to work with me? Won't they just do everything themselves instead?

If I give away my best ideas for free, won't my competitors steal them from me?

Let's address these two concerns separately.

Look at this simple example. If I google "how to fix a leaking sink," there are about 115,000 videos from which I can learn.

Wait. If this how-to, step-by-step information is available for free, shouldn't every single plumber in the world be out of business right now? Of course not. Why is that?

Customers will pay a service-based business for one or all three of these things:

To save time

To hold someone else accountable

To ensure proper execution

Here's the not-so-obvious part about #1 that may assuage your concerns about sharing your expertise freely: If someone has both the time available to learn from you and the time to actually do the work, he or she wasn't going to become your customer anyway. Stop worrying about the people who will never become your customers and start serving the people who will.

Back to that leaky sink: Let's say you're a do-it-yourselfer and you decide to follow a how-to video and invest the time to fix the problem. Congratulations! You did it. Uh-oh. The sink starts leaking again two days later. Whose problem is it? Yours.

When someone exchanges money for your services, they want to mentally check that task off of their list. They need to transfer the ownership of that problem to you. How can you let your prospective customers know they can trust you do this work? You share exactly how to do it. You prove—beyond any doubt in their mind—that you are capable and proficient. Let them know they can hold you accountable for the execution.

Let's think about that book publisher again. What if you reply, "How about we wait until my second book to share the really good stuff?"

Do you think she'd be okay with that? Of course not.

When you're not sharing your very best ideas, you're admitting two things:

You're fearful that there's a finite amount of opportunities. You own your little slice of the marketplace, and you're going to fight off anyone trying to take it from you.

You feel like you've reached your peak. You've stopped learning and developing new ideas, and you're just coasting through life. A year from now, or even a decade from now, you'll still be stuck with the same thinking as you were when you read this in 2017.

What should you do? Understand that there are more opportunities to serve customers than you could ever handle. Stop worrying about people who would never become your customers. Stop worrying about your competition (who, by the way, will never become your customers).

By the time your competitors get around to trying the ideas you've shared, you'll have advanced to the next level, leaving an ever-increasing gap they'll never be able to close.

What's one of the best things about digital and social media? Once you create something, it can be replicated an infinite amount of times without loss of quality.

People will learn from you on their own time without taking any of yours. People will grow to trust you through your shared expertise. People will become your customers because they want you to own their problem.

> *When you educate your prospective customers, you're exchanging something free (information) for something priceless (trust). Break all the rules and start giving away the store.*

Chapter 11

66

"I not only use all of the brains I have, but all that I can borrow and I have borrowed a lot..."

-Woodrow Wilson

99

In the time management portion of this bold business book, we went over what you can do not only to save time, but also to use it more wisely. One of the best ways to save your time is to use someone else's, perhaps an employee's or an outsourced contractor's.

This is what I refer to as a multiplier. A multiplier is a means to multiply what can be done and how you can be compensated that is outside of a practically finite resource. As an example, time for you is a finite resource. What can you do to multiply what you can accomplish in an hour? Naturally, you can get other people to do some of your work. Multipliers help you multiply your accomplishments.

Another way to multiply your success is through residual income. I discovered residual income when I was working for a fire and burglar alarm installation company. I was doing some math on the profit margins of installing alarm systems to figure out a proper raise to ask for. The profit margins seemed awfully low. Then I learned that the alarm systems were sold with a monthly subscription fee for the monitoring and maintenance.

But there wasn't really any maintenance to speak of. It was like buying oil changes for life for an electric car. The customers were paying for peace of mind. To be fair, they were buying an alarm system, so they knew exactly what they were purchasing. The monitoring portion was taken care of by an outsourced company that also offered alarm monitoring for other alarm installers. The alarm installing company received a healthy cut of the monthly subscription fee.

This meant that if we installed an alarm system for a few thousand dollars and the monthly fee was routinely paid, my boss was earning a big portion of the monitoring and maintenance fees every month, presumably forever. Or at least until another alarm system was installed. That got me thinking, and it opened up opportunities to negotiate a higher raise.

Think about landlords and the rent they collect. Think about membership websites. Think about software as a service, a model that the Adobe suite of products has moved to in recent years. Microsoft Office has also gone that direction. Even Amazon has subscriptions to purchase routinely used products such as vitamins and diapers. Consider magazine and newspaper subscriptions or your cable and cell phone bills. Even Clark Griswold became a member of the Jelly of the Month Club in Christmas Vacation. Like Cousin Eddie pointed out to Clark, that's the gift that keeps on giving.

How many times do you work to sell something that is a one-time purchase? How many times do you need to sell something to get someone to pay you routinely forever? The point is that the sales processes for a one-time payout and a recurring

185

payout are essentially the same. You might as well find a way to sell something that can offer you residual income.

Another way to create a multiplier is with content and intellectual property. You could write a book as awesome as this bold business book. Write a song, record a song, write a play, create an invention. In Stephen Key's book, *One Simple Idea*, he details the basics of creating inventions and bringing them to market or having somebody else do the manufacturing while you make residual income off of each sale. There are many options for getting a multiplier of income from intellectual property.

> "I would rather earn 1% of a 100 people's efforts than 100% of my own efforts."
> -J. Paul Getty

Let's explore music as a multiplier. You could write and record a song and get paid nothing immediately. The hope is that when you write this song and record it, you'll sell it. You will lose money until you hit a threshold. That threshold is probably the sale of a few thousand songs. Beyond those, you begin to earn and have cleared a path to income using your intellectual property as a multiplier.

Books offer the same possibility. If you write a book, it costs you (a lot of) money and time. If you sell that book for a few bucks to a few million people, you'll have made an investment that'll pay off well. The same is true of movies and software.

Other areas of opportunity for finding your income multiplier is through affiliate networks and simply offering ads for products on any medium you rent or own. Advertisers use this multiplier effect to create income from nothing. You and I are willing to pay these advertisers because they offer a service that can increase our income. The internet has created so many opportunities for targeted advertising that the entire advertising landscape is still changing.

Consider the irony of a radio station marketing on a billboard. A radio station wants listeners so it can sell airtime to advertisers. To get listeners, the radio station has to market itself to the masses, and billboards are a way to do that in a local area. So the radio station is essentially paying to advertise so that it can get paid for advertising. Crazy, right?

The challenge is to find something to offer your potential clients that gets them excited to buy and you excited to sell. I may be able to make a bunch of cash off energy drinks and cigarettes, but my passion doesn't really lie there. So the money that I'd make wouldn't make up for the pain of dealing with the business. I'd become the kind of a business owner that I don't appreciate.

That, of course, is why you see business owners working day in and day out for their businesses, which is a quandary for some entrepreneurs. You are passionate about what you do and all the people you help. However, as you do this, your business is taking its toll on you in the form of less-than-stellar profits or way too many hours spent working or both. You are not using a multiplier.

Most business owners want more time, more money and more fun. Who doesn't? The bold business owner finds the best solution to solve this familiar and expected quandary in a way that fits his or her desires. Naturally, a business owner's desires may change over time, so a willingness to follow suit and adapt with the dream is important. Find a multiplier that can get you the success you want by getting you both money in your pocket and time available for you spend it.

Another option to resolve this inner conflict of passion is to set up a multiplier to get you some routine income and then do what you love outside of that. Money makes the world go 'round, so you need it. Maybe you can use that cash to get your real dreams fired up and moving.

Whatever you do, make sure you have a reason for doing it. You do not want to be the business owner that people steer clear of because you're constantly chasing the mighty dollar. We like to see others passionate about something. We also love to buy from passionate people. It's one way to all but guarantee that whatever they're selling is great.

If you need a reminder of what passion can do, think of how many presidents were elected because they showed passion. People voted against their beliefs and desires and voted for passion. It's bizarre how focused energy and passion can lead masses to you.

> "You have no right to manage others if you are not passionate about what you do."
> -Bill Quiseng

The opposite of passion is lethargy. Do you really want to run a business that is dull, lifeless and leaves you unfulfilled? Even if your pockets are full, you must have fulfillment in order to be successful. Otherwise you are just another whining business owner. Your business deserves to have your passion built into it as you constantly continue to add passion to it.

Free Time Lunch

I recently sat in on a customer appreciation lunch for the construction industry at a local retail home improvement store. I sat next to a few business owners who were lone wolves in small business. They each had their own truck, hammer, and business name. None had any employees, opting instead for the occasional subcontractor. They were very happy with living on the edge of survival without even knowing it.

Since they didn't have any employees, they were pressed for time. That one-hour lunch could be calculated to have cost them their hourly rate, $50-$100 or so. They chatted about missing phone calls and not getting back to people because, "I was pretty busy last week." I was in the midst of the bastions of customer service, as you can clearly tell. Ironically, they had time to chat for a while that day. Hardly bold business owners, though they seemed to be happy.

In my view, these self-employed job owners were limiting their success by failing to understand the value of employees as well as the need to offer excellent customer service. Without these two key elements, they owned fairly troubling jobs. That sounds terrible, doesn't it?

Lessons Learned: You Are Only as Good as Your (Hired) Team

Richard Branson said it best when he said, "Clients do not come first. Employees come first. If you take care of your employees, they will take care of your clients." Truer words have rarely ever been spoken.

Outsourcing and Employees

You need employees. Get over the head trash of not wanting employees; the right employees will empower, guide, and help grow you as a person. The fact that they will make you money and contribute to your business's success makes it an even sweeter deal.

You have the same 24 hours in your day as everybody else, so you can only accomplish a finite amount of work each day. Presuming you eat, sleep, shower, and spend weekends away from work, you could maybe muster a 12-hour day, 5 days a week. That would net you 60 hours of working time. If you bill out at $100 per hour for every single hour, your maximum revenue is $312,000. That's pretty decent money, but it will cost you your social life and probably your health and well-being.

To make that math accurate, we need to deduct some of the costs of doing business. Is it possible that the actual profit from a business bringing in $300K is more like $150K or lower?

Then the questions of reality come up. How long can you keep up 60 hours per week? How often would you want to? How often do you bill every single hour you work? Even most attorneys struggle to do that. Everybody needs to chat, eat, and pee at some point during the work day.

> "The best executive is one who has sense enough to pick good people to do what he wants done, and self-restraint enough to keep from meddling with them while they do it."
> -Theodore Roosevelt

If you have an employee that you can bill out at $100 per hour and you pay them $25 an hour, you'll net $75 per hour on their work. Let's even add another $30 to that initial $25 to cover overhead costs of truck, office, computer, phone, tools, etc. You'll still net $45 from every hour they bill. If they work 40 hours and bill 75% of their working hours (30 hours), that'll net you over $40,000 annually. If you had to guess, would you believe the one-man armies you meet day to day are making more than $40,000 per year? Probably not. And they are working very hard in miscellaneous fits and starts for whatever they are earning.

On top of the annual income potential from employees, you also have the value they add to your business. For example, the one-man army would have a tough time selling their business. Would you buy a business that was essentially a job?

When it comes to hiring employees, your job is to understand your weaknesses and to hire people who have strengths in those areas. If you're terrible at math, hire a math whiz. If you aren't great at customer service, hire an employee that excels with customers.

Some businesses may believe they are immune to a chapter like this because they already have employees. They already outsource some things. Outsourcing some things in business is essentially automatic. Accounting, IT, and payroll are easily outsourced. The trouble is that some business owners cheap out in other areas that may need outsourcing or hiring. Just because you delegate a bit does not mean that you delegate enough. You need to be able to remove yourself from the business, remember?

No One Can Do It Like I Do It

Have you ever known someone who seems to be sick all the time? That person who always seems to have a cold, even in August? We wonder one of two things: What are they doing wrong? or What are the rest of us are doing right? Maybe it's just allergies, you know, 11 months of the year.

I run into a lot of small businesses that seem to be routinely ill as well, only it's not pollen, cats, or hanging out at daycares. I often see cases of NOCDILIDI (pronounced knock-dill-eye-dee). While this business illness is on the verge of becoming an epidemic, it's rarely contagious. So what is this mystery illness?

NOCDILIDI is an acronym for "No One Can Do It Like I Do It." It means that, as a small business owner, you believe that you do it best. It, of course, may include anything from the creation of the product, to execution of the service, and all of the back-end stuff that goes with the delivery of it. The list of back-end stuff is itself huge, which leads to feeling overwhelmed, the primary symptom of NOCDILIDI. There simply is not enough time in the day for one person to do it all, but they firmly believe that no one can do it like they do it.

For diagnostic purposes, NOCDILIDI has two very prominent and recognizable strains. The first is the insatiable urge to not let go of any work within your business—paperwork, phone calls, emails, scheduling, feedback, social media, sales and marketing, and the actual service or product you sell as well. The list is practically endless. This strain is typically rooted in fear of the unknown or possible failure or fallout from having delegated the tasks to someone else.

 Have a great business growth story? Share it with me!

The second strain is powerful and tough to fight. It's rooted in the reason why many people start a business in the first place. They want to be the boss, want to be needed, and have little time for mopping up other people's messes. Yet mopping up their own messes due to being overwhelmed fits very nicely into their 80-hour work week. They assume that outsourcing to-do list items to others, such as an employee or outsourced vendor, is for the lazy. You can always tell this second strain because the business will be a solid one-person operation that has been operating for more than a decade.

But all this talk of illness is no good unless a cure is presented. So, let me be so bold as to offer those of you suffering from NOCDILIDI a simple tip: **No one cares.**

No one cares that no one can do it like you do it because most people are not aware of how good you think can do it. Some might not even agree with your assessment of how well you do it. They just want it done. Most people couldn't care less if a chimpanzee did it. They may even pay a little extra to see that happen. The full cure is to get systems in place, get your business organized, and get others to do many of the things that currently only you do.

After the sale, the service, and the exchange of money, customers want just one thing: to be happy they bought from you because their need was satisfied. Maybe you fixed a leaky pipe, painted a wall, or remodeled a kitchen. The end result is all they want. I might add that they want it as easily and quickly possible. The last thing a good customer wants is some panting business owner looking like he just ran a marathon pounding through the service they paid for while he takes calls from other customers. NOCDILIDI can scare customers away if it goes untreated. At best, you'll have to be the cheapest in town to keep customers.

Most business owners, at some time, have had a case of NOCDILIDI. Eliminate the NOCDILIDI and watch your business flourish as your freedom and profit blossom.

The multiplier effect will help your additions

Lessons Learned: Opportunity Costs

Every business has a life cycle. Each business will wallow in certain areas of their lifecycle based on the values, awareness, and actions of the leadership. What must be considered is the opportunity cost for each action or expenditure. A dollar spent here means that that dollar cannot be spent elsewhere. Time is the same way, though on a much more finite scale.

Cash is King

Another multiplier is the cash multiplier. A cash multiplier can be a savings account, CD, money market, or even a mutual fund. There are dozens of options that you can utilize to multiply your money over time. Avoid storing it under your mattress or spending it on something that you know you can't sell for more than you paid for it. Be aware of the opportunity cost of the money that you aren't multiplying. Also have some cash available for the sweet business bargains that come along that only cash can help you to execute.

Realistically though, this is a bold business book, not an investment book. What you do with the truckloads of cash your business brings in is your business.

> *"Money looks better in the bank than on your feet."*
> -Sophia Amoruso

Multiply and Conquer

To be a bold business owner you need to have a multiplier to get yourself more time and more money. If you have employees and do what you can to remove yourself from being necessary in your business, you have a worthwhile business to sell. The employee(s) make you money year after year as well as helping to give value to your business for when you exit. This a beautiful

Chapter 12

"
*"If you just communicate, you can get by. But if you
communicate skillfully, you can work miracles."*
-Jim Rohn
"

When communicating with anyone, you must make them
feel like you understand their needs, wants and emotions. Even if
in the off chance you really don't care. You just need the people
you are communicating with to feel like you care.

If you have ever been to a rock concert and heard the star
shout out, "How are you feeling tonight?" Do you believe they truly
care? Deep down inside we feel they do, because we can watch as
the intensity of the crowd builds up as a response. Of course, the
loud whistles and "Woo!" shouts proclaim that more than a few
people believe this rock star truly cares. The concert goers have
given meaning to the question, and the rock star understands this.
Your job is to be a rockstar, in your own special way.

Communication Breakdown

Although communication is the driving force of business, it is rarely spoken about since we live in a world full of communication devices. With all of this technology, the assumption might be that we have this communication thing down pat. How often do you find yourself looking up from your keyboard or phone only to see the great majority of people still looking down at their devices?

From all of this technology we, as a society, have seemingly suffered. We do not have better communication; we simply have more communication. The problem is that most communication only flows one way—the worst type of communication. It's like reading a book you cannot reply to. (Reply back to james@ drawincustomers.com.)

Phone calls, texting, emails, social media chat, and a plethora of other evolving tools of communication are causing a lot of chaos in our orderly little world. Let's dive into the best ways to communicate in business.

Phone Calls

Since I have a receptionist service, this mode of communication is dear to me. However, I define our company as a communication business, rather than a phone business. As other means of communicating become the norm, we will adapt as needed. The phone is just so simple, quick, and effective that it would be sad to have it go away anytime soon.

Do you answer your business phone? I don't mean "usually" or "sometimes" or "pretty often." I mean all the time. Sure, you may miss a call or two when you meet the delivery person at the door, but is that the norm or only on a rare occasion?

I asked these questions to a potential client. He ran a high-end remodeling and construction business. His company would not build a house for less than $500,000, which, where I live in Wisconsin, is a pretty nice house. When I asked him if he was missing calls, he stated matter-of-factly, "It is accepted in our industry that we will not always answer the phone. We may not even get back to you, ever." As you can imagine, I was taken aback. Who runs a business that expects customers to call multiple times to hopefully get you on a good day when you accidentally answer your phone? Especially when working with higher-end clients?

I countered in the way that I do when I know I'm not going to make the sale and asked, "Would it make sense that if I had $1 million dollars to spend on a house and I got your cell phone voicemail, I would call the next builder?" His reply was a quaint "probably."

So here is a guy who knows that he is losing business by not having his phone answered. It makes you wonder how other business owners perceive their clients. I guess if you, as a customer, are able to get through to a business, the stars have aligned in everyone's favor.

Answering the phone is the first step. Getting a friendly person to answer your business phone is a whole new opportunity for failure or great success. I set up my first business to be the pinnacle of customer service. Part of that was answering the phone in a friendly tone and doing everything we could to help the caller as fast as we could. That is the beauty of phone calls. You don't need 20 minutes to schedule something. It can be done in mere seconds on the phone. Add in a quick "hello" and "see you later," and your job is complete.

Lessons Learned: Auto Attendants Are Ridiculous

Whoever invented the auto-attendant was thinking as a business and not as a consumer. At one point, I had an auto-attendant answer my phones. Every button press got the caller to me or my voicemail eventually. It was useless, selfish, and unnecessary. Especially if your auto-attendant has customers enter data they need to give to the operator who eventually answers anyway. Client time wasted is client trust lost.

How to be an Outstanding Receptionist
by Lacie Lederman, Calls On Call
callsoncall.com

Anyone can be a receptionist. Though becoming an outstanding receptionist takes a lot of hard work and experience that will develop over time. What are the most important traits of an outstanding receptionist? Let's find out.

1. Exceptional Phone Voice and Manner
Anybody can learn how to answer the phone, but having a "phone voice" is a powerful skill. It has to do with pitch and stressing of syllables and sounding like you genuinely care. Always be polite and respectful to each and every caller. Take accurate notes of correct caller details, and repeat telephone numbers if necessary for return calls.

2. Terrific Listener
You need to listen to what the client is telling you and respond with a solution. You may have the information they want, with this information easily accessible to allow you to promptly assist them.

3. Wonderful Sense of Humor
It really helps for a receptionist to see the funny side of life and to make clients feel welcome while waiting.

4. Dazzling Wardrobe
All receptionists should dress well and wear a welcoming bright smile. A receptionist is usually the first person a customer sees when they cross the doorstep into your office.

> *Like I mentioned, anyone can be a receptionist. But being an outstanding receptionist takes a lot of skill and practice. You need the right attitude and genuinely care for your clients.*

Emails

Emails are one of the more challenging forms of communication. For now, let's just mention that businesses and customers like emails because things are in writing, convenient, and less interruptive than phone calls. But they also take longer for a conversation and leave many discussions without immediate closure. Emails have a tendency to be held hostage in your mind and your inbox, taking up valuable space that could be used for much more productive things.

Business Email Etiquette

Have you ever sent an email that mentioned an attachment but failed to actually attach something? Some email programs look for keywords like attachment to prevent you from making this simple mistake. What is the protocol for dropping the ball on something so simple and common? Let's look at some business etiquette, shall we?

When you send an email that should have an attachment and you forget to actually attach something, it makes you look silly at first. Maybe you realize it right after you hit send. Maybe the recipient asks you for the attachment. This can result in one of two reactions.

The first possible reaction is that you both laugh, acknowledging that this is a common error. You apologize and resend the email joking about the silly mistake. You can use simple phrases in your apologetic email such as "This attachment was so important it took me two emails to send it," or "I wanted to verify you check your email promptly. Good Job!" The appropriateness of these responses depends on your relationship with the recipient.

The second reaction is a stern reply from the recipient that belittles you for failing in such a simple capacity. Certainly this stern reply is from someone who has never forgotten to attach something to an email. This person also never leaves toast crumbs in the butter, always signals before a lane change, and flosses at least twice a day. Regardless, it's best to apologize in your reply and attach the necessary attachment. Forgetting twice is just bad form.

You may need to avoid joking with some people. They typically have stern brows and cost you a lot of money. Jokes take time, and if misunderstood, they can bring about unintended consequences. Generally speaking, the world can use a good chuckle. Just be careful.

Respect the Reply

As a business owner who uses email constantly, I am often reminded of the simple law of communication. That law states that communication, by definition, needs to have at least two parties sharing information with each other. Without getting all philosophical, if an email is read but not replied to, is it truly communication?

Have you ever read an email and not responded? I'm not talking about spam; I'm talking about the emails from individuals asking for a specific response, emails that contain information and, often, a question. Something along the lines of, "Will you be going to this?"

When you do not reply, both you and the sender are making some interpretations. Those interpretations may be that technology failed them and that the email is in the spam folder or never made it into the appropriate inbox. It may also be interpreted that a big fat no doesn't necessitate a reply or that a no reply means a big fat no. Or perhaps the sender thinks that you simply haven't gotten to the message yet. You see, email is one of those ways of communication that can have a delay in response, therefore, a delayed response can be interpreted in many ways.

You should respond to all emails addressed to you

individually, presuming a question was asked. If you do not, you risk alienating the sender. This alienation may lead to emotional turmoil or to the sender just not liking you. Senders know people and you get business from people.

You may fail to respond to an email since your inbox has a scroll bar. But whatever the reason, you are automatically sending a message that states, "I do not respect you." There is respect in a reply. It takes a few seconds for most replies, so the time excuse is invalid.

> ### Lessons Learned: Email Inboxes Should Not Have a Scroll Bar
>
> If your inbox is that full, you need to clean it up. That mess will only add baggage to your day. Email inbox zero is achievable. Visit http://drawincustomers.com/how-to-get-to-email-inbox-zero/

This goes back to the definition of communication. Is communication happening if a reply is expected and not received? I suppose when you shout into a canyon and you hear the echo, you could claim you were communicating. Oddly, that's not too far off from how some people in business communicate. Even outside of business, come to think of it.

Reply All

If ever in the history of buttons there was one button that was pushed too often, it is the Reply All button. Maybe the second floor button on an elevator beats Reply All, but it's close. How many times have you seen an email come to you that was addressed to a pile of other people? Quite a few, I imagine. And how many times have you also received a reply from one of the initial recipients that sent out a reply to everyone on the sender's list that had absolutely nothing to do with you or more than one of the other recipients. They go like this:

Initial Email:

> Hi All,
> We are having a party this Saturday starting at 7pm. Bring some stuff.
> -Tracy the Party Person

Reply All:

> Sorry, I cannot make it. I am having knee surgery after finding out that those spores on my back have started to open, and the doctors are not sure if it is contagious. The doctors say I will be fine in a few months but that I should limit the partying to four times per week.
> -Jesse the Reply All-er

Clearly, Jesse has some other issues she may have wanted to share in a bizarre way. The point is that Jesse was assuming the entire crowd cared that: 1) she was not coming to the party, and 2) her spore issues had some progress. I dare say that both are incorrect assumptions.

There are times that Reply All is useful. For example, if the email is addressed to two other people, for a total of three in communication with each other. The main idea is to use your discretion. Don't fill up people's inboxes with your unnecessary Reply All responses.

How Long?

Email is a great way to communicate if for nothing other than leaving a digital paper trail. One of the challenges with email, however, is the length of the message. Effective communication is two-way, and long emails are rarely appropriate in two-way conversations.

Also, while many emails look completely normal on a computer, they can look like small novels on a cell phone. It doesn't matter how big your cell phone screen is. If it fits in a pocket, that screen can barely hold 200 words. Is it OK for the reader to scroll to get your point? Sometimes yes, often no.

Desired Outcomes

When you draft an email to someone, you have a desired outcome in mind, whether it is to set up a meeting, get an answer to a question, or have the recipient react in some other way. What you must include in your email is a direct call to action to limit the need for many back and forth responses based on your desired outcome.

For example, asking in your email if you want to meet for coffee sometime and not offering potential times and places will lead to additional emails with questions that could have been addressed in the initial email. Side note: Be sure to mark suggested options down in your calendar as potential meetings with this person. Use Boomerang or a similar service to make sure you get a response, and follow-up if you do not.

Send Later

Some emails you have time to write now, although they may be best sent in an hour or a week. With the scheduled delivery option on most email programs, you can time your emails to be sent at the most opportune moments.

Test Send

If you are sending an important email and you have a moment, it makes sense to send it to yourself as a test. I like to send test emails using a delayed send feature. That way I almost get surprised when I am pounding through my inbox and see a message that I can read and judge the tone from. Then when I realize it is from me I can fix if needed with no harm done. Just remember to actually send the important email when you are done testing.

> *"The single biggest problem in communication is the illusion that it has taken place."*
> -George Bernard Shaw

Text

If ever the world has failed in its adaptation of a communication medium, text messaging is it. Cave drawings have more uses than texts. Texting is good for only three things: 1) yes-no answers to simple questions, 2) wasting time, and 3) stealthy communication. If you have a business, you should not be interested in #2. If you have a mistress, texts may be your saving grace. If you have a simple question, texts are fantastic. If you want to schedule something, texts offer a great way to spend the next two hours establishing a time and place.

Phone calls remove body language from communication, which plays a huge part of excellent communication. Texts remove body language, tone and, for some people, coherence. That red squiggly line under your words does not mean good job. It means if you click SEND before addressing them, you are contributing to the downfall of our society. Plus car accidents. Seriously, no one wants to talk to you that badly. It can wait.

> *"People have entire relationships via text message now, but I am not partial to texting. I need context, nuance and the warmth and tone than can only come from a human voice."*
> -Danielle Steel

Social Media

Social media is continuously evolving as a communication medium. Some business people use the chat function on Facebook or other outlets to get in front of people right away. In my mind, this is as annoying as texting. It is in your face and bugs you until you respond. Which leads to further inefficient communication. Maybe I am old, but communicating in business the same way a 12-year-old chats with her friends seems silly to me. That said, some clients use it, which means that you, as a business owner, will have to adapt. Communicate with the customer in the way the customer wants to communicate.

> *"Don't use big words.*
> *They mean so little."*
> Oscar Wilde

Online Chat

Online chat has its benefits. You can juggle chatting and doing other work. Also, many of these modes of communication are for people who are simply unwilling to talk to a person over the phone when they have a question or need some help. Often chat is seen as easier to work with. With online chat you can offer website links, cookie-cutter instructions and the ability to save or forward the conversation. If you have the means to maintain an online chat portal, it is recommended.

> *"The most important thing in*
> *communication is hearing*
> *what isn't said."*
> -Peter Drucker

In Person

Huh? Who does that?

You may come across a potential client who is actually in your presence—flesh and blood and looking to spend money with you. Be nice, say hello, and use please and thank you. Compliment them on something, ask how business is going, and be genuinely sincere in your questions. Real human interaction is severely lacking in our world. (And don't you dare pick up your phone when you're speaking with someone.) Pick up on body language signals that tell you what the other person wants to hear.

I'm a volunteer for Big Brothers Big Sisters. My 16-year-old little brother had a rough time communicating, unless you were chatting about Call of Duty. Then he got himself a job at a mall food stand. In less than two weeks, that kid could talk with anyone about anything. He looked up and made eye contact. He moved his head in understanding and acknowledgement. He used his body to communicate cheerfully instead of responding all mopey-like. Do you know why? He was working for tips. People don't usually tip jerks with poor communication skills. He learned to make their food choice and interaction with him the highlight of their day. What if he were a grown up with a business? Imagine the possibilities.

Networking 101

You need to know people in order to sell to people, right? The first step is simple. You need to learn how to network. Period.

I attended a presentation on networking a couple years ago. I mistakenly thought it was going to be a speed-networking event; I could meet a bunch of people and move along with my life. But, it turned out to be a "How to Network" educational seminar. The irony was that, as people came in, they sat down and stared at their phones. Zero human interaction was happening outside of me talking to a few people around me.

As it turned out, this presentation was geared for a different age bracket than mine and focused on a different business demographic. While the suggestions that were given were relatively entry-level, the attendees seemed genuinely interested in improving their basic networking skills. But all of the silence in that crowd leads me to the first rule of networking.

Talk to People.

It seems so obvious that I wouldn't have believed it even

needed to be stated. But after a recent visit to a startup camp for young programmers, I'm convinced it truly does need to be mentioned. I understand that, for some, talking to new people is uncomfortable if not downright terrifying. But, I assure you, talking to people is easy. Simply walk up to someone and say something like, "Hi, my name is James. You look like one of the smartest people here." That should get a conversation going. If it doesn't, then you need to consider the second rule of networking.

Don't Stink.

I say this on a humid, 90-degree July afternoon. If you have been outside for more than five minutes, you probably stink. If you're at an outdoor networking event, you shouldn't worry too much. If it's an indoor event, that's a different story. No one cares if you use the most natural of natural soaps you can find. If you stink or sweat like a cold beer, people probably won't want to hang out by you.

People use all of their senses when you approach them. Your smile should hit them first, then your eyes, then your scent, then your handshake. Your scent should be good but not overpowering. Too much perfume or cologne is almost as bad as terrible body odor. Almost.

Imagine you're at a networking event and you are not smiling, refuse to make eye contact, and smell funny. You'll have a challenging time meeting people and a worse time making a good impression. People are there to meet people, introduce people, and judge people. It's simply what people do when they are in groups of any kind, right?

Show Up.

You've probably had days when you were just beat. You'd spent the last ten hours chatting with the world, hustling deals, solving problems, beating away emails and phone calls, putting out fires, and then the time came for you to hop in your car and go meet more new people. (So that when those new contacts bloomed into business relationships, you could chat, hustle, solve, beat, and put out more fires.)

On such days, your decision could have been to go home and nurture your family relationships a bit, which is a fine answer. Your decision could have been to go home and watch TV, which probably wouldn't make you any more successful. Your decision could have also been to hit the networking event for an hour, chill out for a bit, and see if you can't find that one powerful influencer to bring you in the easy money business.

More often than not, whenever I choose to hit the networking event, I'm happy I did. The first thing I do is get in line to grab a beer and meet others there. It's the easiest thing in the world to talk to people waiting for beer. They all need something to help them pass the time. It might as well be them telling you about themselves and you telling them a bit about yourself and your business.

The fifth rule of networking is also simple.

Meet Somebody.

How many times have you gone to an event filled with dozens or hundreds of people, and you stayed in your corner chatting with the same cronies you always hang with? Or you stared at your phone like you were waiting for the Go/No Go order from your secret agent partner? Go meet somebody new. Ask your friends to introduce you or just walk up to a person who looks interesting. How did you meet the friends you have now?

I use a tactic from a pickup artist. (Believe me, you can find useful sales and psychology information in the craziest places.) He tells his fellow picker-uppers that they have three seconds to talk to a girl from the first moment they spot her. When networking, use the same rule. You make a move to talk to a person who looks interesting within three seconds of seeing them. The three-second rule eliminates the hesitancy that arises in situations in which you feel you are in danger, such as jumping out of a plane or going on stage to speak. You can use this rule for all kinds of things. Need to have a conversation with an employee? You have three seconds to initiate it.

Pickup artists and networking professionals use the same body language and similar rules. When you are at a networking event and want to meet someone, you are essentially like a pickup artist looking for a date. You're just interested in selling them something or getting them to sell for you rather than sleeping with them. (Hopefully that's not too big of an assumption for you.)

You can add to the rules if it makes you more comfortable. I know people who have a five-card rule. You must hand your business card to at least five people, then you are free to leave. Or the one-hour rule. Talk to as many people as possible in an hour, then you are free to go.

Optional rules for networking events:
- Give out five business cards.
- Collect five business cards.
- Invite at least two people to coffee.
- Shake hands with at least 20 people.
- Network for at least one hour.
- Collect more business cards than your partner.
- Introduce three people you just met to other people.
- Keep moving to the back of the beer line as you make conversations with those in line.
- High-five at least four people.
- Borrow at least five pens.
- Make a $1 bet with someone new.
- Have a conversation with someone and slowly step backwards in a circle. Complete the circle before moving on.
- Take three selfies with people you just met. Post them on social media.
- Ask three people for advice on your business card/ logo/website/etc.
- Talk to five people that _____ .

In the end, after you attend a few networking events, it gets easier and more fun. I hated them when I first started going because I knew no one and some of the events I went to were pretty lame. But they were lame because I let them be lame. I could have made them great. I just didn't realize it at the time. If only I would have read The Bold Business Book sooner... The sixth rule of networking is to watch what you eat.

Avoid Finger Food.

I'm not sure how this happens. People will be shaking hands and talking at these events, and the host will have nachos or some other finger food. I typically avoid the food altogether. It's not easy to hold a drink, balance a plate of food, shake hands, and talk like you mean it. I talk with my hands a lot, so that makes matters worse.

If you are truly there for the free food, enjoy. But my job at a networking event is to meet people. The opportunity cost for other people I could be spending time with both in the room and elsewhere is too great for me to care about deviled eggs or cold pizza. If you weren't networking, what would you be doing? Because you have decided to network, you are giving up something. Time with your family, friends or relaxation time. Make sure the trade-off is worth it.

Often people equate attendance to a networking event with actual networking. Much like attending a marathon but not actually going for a run, it takes more than just showing up to be successful. Though it is a good start.

The final rule of networking is the golden rule of networking.

Work Harder to Introduce Than to be Introduced.

The world revolves around strong relationships and communication. Without these, we'd have a very lonely planet. You probably don't want a lonely planet. You want a bustling planet. Unless it's after 9 p.m. Then be quiet, you have an early

209

morning tomorrow.

The more you help others, the more others will be compelled to help you. Think of what Tom and Sue can accomplish with that introduction. Once you become well connected, you become an influencer. An influencer is someone you want to be.

People want to know and be liked by an influencer because an influencer can move mountains for others. An influencer does this through contacts. Influencers only stay influencers when they maintain great contacts and share them. When you have conversations that lead you to introduce people to people, you are on your way to becoming an influencer. As an influencer, your sphere is so large that people know you know people, and they know you won't introduce them to someone you don't trust, whether it be roofing, insurance, real estate, pest control, or whatever.

That's powerful because as an influencer you are helping the world. Basically you are the bold business owner that people go to when they need someone who "knows a guy." That will build trust, which is something that needs to be earned.

It is best to understand that networking is a give and be given game. If you send me a client, I will feel the desire to send a client back to you. If you send me ten clients, I will do anything I can to get you as many clients as I can. This works well in both directions. So if I give you ten clients, what will you want to do for me?

You need to forget the mindset that you are networking only for you. Networking is for the good of all in the network (at least the ethical members of the network), so your job is to work on connecting people.

Networking is something I believe people should do regardless of where they are professionally. Everyone is in sales, so it pays to know as many people as possible. It pays more to be known by as many people as possible. You cannot do either if you do not get out and meet people.

You have many ways to connect people after you meet them. A phone call or email is a great way to get connections made. I like phone calls because it gives me a chance to catch up with people I haven't spoken to in a while. It's great to get my ear on the pulse of business by speaking with old contacts.

Email has its advantages as well. It gives everyone something tangible to look at, file, and react to if they choose. The information is right there in an easily searchable format. Plus, your email signature with your logo gets in front of a couple people.

Introductions

Here is an example of a cookie-cutter email I like to send to connect people:

Joe,
I would like to introduce you to <Mary Jane>. <Mary> owns <Awesome Company>, an enterprising business that helps people <do awesome things>. Mary is looking for <something Joe offers>.

Mary's contact info is:
Mary Jane
Awesome Company Inc.
mary@awesomecompanyinc.com
555-456-7890

Mary,
I would like to introduce you to <Joe Business>. Joe is a <title> at <Another Awesome Company>, a prominent <true compliment>. Joe is always looking for people looking for <things that Mary is looking for>. It would be worth reaching out to <Joe> to have a conversation.

Joe's contact info:
Joe Business
Another Awesome Company
joe@anotherawesomecompany.com

555-765-4321

I have copied both of you on this email. I will let you take it from here.

Good times!
<Your Name>

Using this template, you can copy both parties and let the email fly. Follow-up if you'd like with either or both parties. Otherwise, let technology do its thing. You did your part and the individual parties will do theirs if they feel compelled.

I also like to use the subject line, "Introductions." It's simple and if the recipients know you, it will definitely be opened. Who wouldn't want to open an email like that?

> *"The value of a man is not measured by what he does for himself to make his life easier, but measured by what he does for others to make their lives easier."*
> -Eric E Thomas

Can you be known by many people? The question is not can you; the question is will you. Your business relies on people to grow and to be known. You also rely on people just to survive. Can you imagine your life with absolutely no one around? It would be pretty difficult.

Human relations is a huge topic; we've only scratched the surface. If I could leave you with just one bit, I would say this: Talk to people. All people. The people you sit next to on a plane, the people in line, the people who work for you. Everyone has a compelling story, even if they don't believe so. You never know who you will talk to who can help you or, more importantly, who you can help.

Follow Up and Through

The biggest mistake a networker can make is not following up with new contacts and not following through on promises that were made to these contacts. Some conversations with new people get deeper and more fulfilling than the networking room can allow. Because you attended this event to meet as many people as possible, you may need to press the pause button and set up a time to meet again to continue the conversation.

The failure comes when you set up that next meeting but don't follow through. You had an insightful conversation that you both agreed would be great on a larger scale, and you blew it. Opportunity lost. The same is true of all of the new contacts you made at your networking event. You collected business cards, shook hands, and went home with a smile and a load of possibilities sailing through your mind. The next day you were overwhelmed with day-to-day life, and, before you know it, two weeks have passed and you still haven't sent an email or called any of the people you met.

Here's the rule: schedule time the day after the networking event to follow up with the contacts you made. It doesn't take long; you can even have a boilerplate email ready. Something like this:

Hi Alan,

It was great to meet you at the <whatever event> yesterday. I hope you were able to make some great connections. It seemed like a good crowd, didn't it?

Based on the pile of business cards I received, I know it's sometimes easy to forget who is who. As a reminder, I was the guy with the <memorable thing>. You mentioned <something worth mentioning>.

Here is my contact info if you are interested in chatting again.

Thanks!

<Your name>

The trick is to use your cookie-cutter email, but take a minute to tweak it so it's a bit more personalized. People want to feel unique and special. So make them feel unique and special. At no point should you not follow up with someone. Even a 12-year-old kid who was joined at the hip to his dad would be great to follow up with. Who knows who that kid knows? He may be your best new client. Treat everyone with respect, and they will do the same for you.

> **"I was hesitant to go around and shake hands, just go up and stick my hand out to strangers. Then I learned to stick my hand out."**
>
> -Jim Edgar

Shake Hands With Everyone You Meet

I have arguably shaken more hands than the president. I have had saggy handshakes and crush-your-fingernails handshakes. A handshake should be firm enough to show you are confident, but loose enough to not be able to take a pulse. A slight touch of the elbow will do wonders as well. A good handshake will let your conversational partner know you are smart, confident, and trustworthy.

> **"I forgot to shake hands and be friendly. It was an important lesson about leadership."**
>
> -Lee Iacocca

Some of the greatest ice-breakers have been when I had my hand at an odd angle, and the handshake ended up being lame. I'd say, "That was a lame handshake, let's try that again." Ice broken, conversation started, and networking continued.

Sometimes when you go to shake a hand, the other person wants a hug. Give them a hug. Make sure you still have your wallet after the hug, but hug on. Hugs are more intimate than handshakes and will serve everyone better. I always go in for the handshake first because I don't like to be the person trying to hug people who are trying to shake hands. But I haven't perfected this yet. If you have tips in that regard, I'm all ears. As it turns out, I am not alone. My "hug radar" is not that great, and, according to the results from a quick question I tossed out on social media, others struggle with this social issue too. Check this out:

James Kademan
July 27 · 🌐 ▼

You may know, I am writing a book. I need some guidance in regards to the handshakes and hugs thing in business. You networkers know what I mean. Comment or message me your insights. www.drawincustomers.com/boldness

👍 Like   💬 Comment   ➴ Share

██████████████████████████████

████████████NO HUGGING!
Unlike · Reply · 👍 1 · July 27 at 4:22pm

████████████████████ If I have known someone for a long time and consider them a friend (even if they are my customer, vendor, etc.), I have no problem giving them a hug. I'm a hugger. It would be awkward to shake their hand. Case in point, had a long time client of ours in the office today, 2 of the people we don't deal with on a more regular basis we shook hands with, the 3rd who we've worked with the longest laughed and said something to the effect of I'm not shaking your hand! - and gave us all hugs. I really think it depends on the personal relationship, and ability to gauge what the other person would deem appropriate.
Unlike · Reply · 👍 3 · July 27 at 4:38pm

████████████████████Don't hug me. It's, at its best awkward and is often uncomfortable.
Unlike · Reply · 👍 1 · July 27 at 4:52pm

██████████████████ I agree with ████████████ While I'm generally not a hugger, if it's someone I've known/worked with for a long time, and THEY are huggers, I'm totally down for a friendly hug.
Unlike · Reply · 👍 1 · July 27 at 5:06pm

215

> ## "The best place in the world is inside a hug."
> -Jota Quest

 [redacted] Oh man. I have had a few awkward moments of thinking people were going in for a hug and it ended up being a very close handshake. I agree with Rachel and Melissa. Depends on where you are and who it is. It's great Oxytocin. 😊

Unlike · Reply · 👍 1 · July 27 at 5:15pm

[redacted] I will pass on the man hug but some of my guy friends do it all the time. I'm ok with the female hug but usually that is more of a friend type relationship than a client. However it does happens a lot in real estate after the closing.

Unlike · Reply · 👍 1 · July 27 at 6:50pm

[redacted] I never hug my clients unless they reach out to hug me, brides tend to be huggers but most people just want a smile and to feel like you are genuinely happy to see them. Also for me personally any one who hugs me I will not see again... Personal space is a big thing... And well I do full body waxing on clients so that's saying something lol

Unlike · Reply · 👍 1 · July 27 at 7:36pm

James Kademan Awesome answers! So I can tell I am not alone in regards to this. Is there some body language tell tale sign to look for?

Like · Reply · July 27 at 8:31pm

[redacted] I can't wait to hug you next time I see you. A great big man hug! 😊

Unlike · Reply · 👍 1 · July 27 at 8:49pm

[redacted] You could just ask

Unlike · Reply · 👍 2 · July 27 at 9:02pm

 James Kademan I love hugs. I am just not into weirding people out too much. Hug on, **[redacted]**!

Like · Reply · 👍 1 · July 28 at 2:09pm

> ## "Too often we underestimate the power of a touch, a smile, a kind word, a listening ear, an honest accomplishment, or the smallest act of caring, all of which have the potential to turn a life around."
> -Leo Buscaglia

████████████████ I agree with ████████████ - I am a hugger but not when it comes to business. However, I've known and worked with Rachel so long, I hug her when I see her. 😊
Unlike · Reply · 👍 2 · July 27 at 8:54pm

████████████████ Hug if worked with them a long time and consider them friends but you have to have a hug radar to know when appropriate
Like · Reply · 👍 1 · July 27 at 9:13pm

████████████████ Hug radar. James - this is he perfect phrase!!
Unlike · Reply · 👍 1 · July 27 at 11:05pm

Like · Reply · July 28 at 8:34am

James Kademan I like it! What does this radar look like?
Like · Reply · July 28 at 2:16pm

████████ 1, hugging are for people you connect with, bond with on a personal level, even though it's business. 2. As for hand shake, 1. Make it real, unless you don't care. If you miss, step forward and insure connection/ respect. 2. Follow number # 1....Unless you don't really give a dam who you're greeting!.
Unlike · Reply · 👍 1 · July 27 at 9:17pm · Edited

████████ "Act like you care even if you dont" - the unfortunate thing is most people suck at this and it can be picked out faster than a fire in a hay field. I think far too often people follow a "procedure" based on similar reasons as one would find in a cosmo mag article entitled: "what not to do on a first date". They're too busy following the "prescription for networking success" that they forget to adapt to the encounter in real time (something humans naturally do well).

No matter the encounter, it must be actually genuine. I love when people try to offend me as its genuine for them, and opens so many doors to dialogue, discourse and debate where when civil, can build an amazing rapport with someone very quickly even if you disagree and stay in disagreement.
Unlike · Reply · 👍 1 · July 28 at 8:14am

████████ Depends on relationship. Business; shake hands. Friend or family first; hug. Surprised nobody mentioned the hand shake/cheek kiss. It's common in some cultures and I encounter it occasionally. This one definitely needs "hug radar" to be done respectfully.
Like · Reply · 👍 1 · July 28 at 8:36am · Edited

████████ http://www.ibmadison.com/.../Shake-hands-or-hug-it-out.../ 😊

Shake hands or hug it out? Embracing awkward moments in business greetings -...
IBMADISON.COM

217

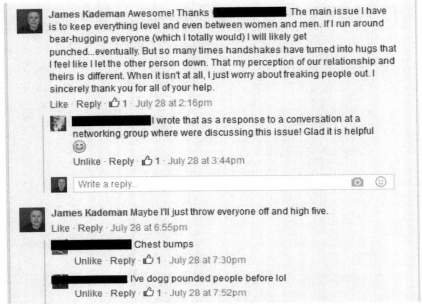

James Kademan Awesome! Thanks ███████████. The main issue I have is to keep everything level and even between women and men. If I run around bear-hugging everyone (which I totally would) I will likely get punched...eventually. But so many times handshakes have turned into hugs that I feel like I let the other person down. That my perception of our relationship and theirs is different. When it isn't at all, I just worry about freaking people out. I sincerely thank you for all of your help.

Like · Reply · 🖒 1 · July 28 at 2:16pm

███████████ I wrote that as a response to a conversation at a networking group where were discussing this issue! Glad it is helpful 😊

Unlike · Reply · 🖒 1 · July 28 at 3:44pm

Write a reply...

James Kademan Maybe I'll just throw everyone off and high five.
Like · Reply · July 28 at 6:55pm

███████████ Chest bumps
Unlike · Reply · 🖒 1 · July 28 at 7:30pm

███████████ I've dogg pounded people before lol
Unlike · Reply · 🖒 1 · July 28 at 7:52pm

The conversation eventually eroded a bit after that. But, the point is that your hug radar is essentially just about reading body language. You'll notice that most of the men who responded to my post were all about handshakes, high fives, and the occasional chest bump. The women's stances reflected the unique position they're in as our society's gender roles continue to evolve into something more equitable.

My rule has been to advance to the highest common denominator. If you go in for a handshake and someone else offers a hug, go with the hug. Vanessa Van Edwards, Lead Investigator at the Science of People, a human behavioral research lab, has videos which clearly show how to move your body with your right hand out for a handshake and your left arm wide for a hug, just in case. For both moves, Vanessa recommends pivoting the arms with the elbows close to your side. Or if you are a big anti-hugger, or the approaching person just ran a marathon, bring both hands directly forward to protect yourself from whatever cooties you are concerned about. In reality, issues like this are great for breaking the ice and laughing at the confusion. Just don't be creepy, and you'll do fine.

As a BOLD Business owner, your job is to go boldly into the introduction and welcome the other person. Your job is to make the other person feel as comfortable as possible. This is why I typically go for a handshake. I have no intention of making anybody feel uncomfortable. It also helps me feel like everyone is on even ground. However, if we meet and you want to hug, I am all for it.

Meeting Her Match

by Rachel Rasmussen, Rescue Desk Virtual Assistant Services
rescuedeskva.com

I am a loyal and dedicated attendee of most of the events hosted by my local chamber of commerce. Once or twice a quarter, the chamber hosts an educational breakfast session with a local speaker who entertains the audience about everything from networking to sales to doing the books.

At an event I attended very early in my career as an entrepreneur, an interesting phenomenon caught me off guard, turning my insides into a rather liberated—albeit it a little confused—pile of squishy mish-mash. My inner introvert lost her first fight. Ever. She NEVER loses a fight! She's calculating and convincing and scrappy. She's quick to remind me that I'm more comfortable laying low doing my own thing, not drawing too much attention to myself. She regularly points out that public recognition shoves me so far out of my comfort zone that I end up with a bruise. But, I think she finally met her match: my inner business owner.

I wandered into that breakfast event, pleasantly surprised to recognize a few faces and pleased to rekindle a few connections. I made my way into the standing-only, 60-person classroom, parked myself toward the back, and settled in for the presentation. I noticed a woman I met at a previous event up in the front of the room, helping the speaker set up. Then, loud enough for God and most of the room to hear, she pointed me out to one of her colleagues. "Hey! That's Rachel! The Rescue Desk lady I told you about! You should meet her!" Not only did her colleague turn to look at me, but so did half the room. In fact, I'm pretty sure the cars driving by outside slowed down to rubberneck. Here's how the 5-second dialogue played out in my head:

Inner Introvert: Ohmigod, ohmigod, everyone's looking at us! Wha'dowedo?! Wha'dowedo?!

Inner Business Owner: Dude, pipe down! This is AWESOME! Lookit all the people who just heard not only your name, but the name of your business! Wooo-hooo!!

Inner Introvert: Ohmigod, ohmigod...but EVERYONE IS LOOKING AT US! WHA'DOWEDO?!

Inner Business Owner: I'll TELL you what we're going to do. We're going to stand up, smile, say hello, shake her hand, and tell her how nice it is to meet her. Then, just because you're a pain in my ass, we're going to smile at everyone else in the damn room.

Inner Introvert: Ohmigod, ohmigod...BUT...BUT...

Inner Business Owner: But nothing! If you don't chill out RIGHT NOW, I swear I'll bust out the business cards and start sending them down this row of strangers.

It's about time my inner introvert got her tail-end handed to her on a platter. It was long overdue.

I think this is a lesson every introverted business owner eventually learns. In fact, no matter what your personality, I think everyone's inner business owner needs to be a little feisty, willing to take whatever heat is necessary to protect a new and growing business. Introvert be damned.

Empathetic Listening to Prevent the Dissing

One of the hardest lessons I've had to learn is empathetic listening. This is probably because I am made up of brutally efficient logic in order to keep the pace I want to keep. Robots don't have feelings, which is one of the reasons they're so good at what they do. I don't need to sweet talk a Roomba to get it to vacuum the floor. It just does it because I told it to.

Humans, on the other hand, definitely have emotions. Time-consuming emotions that need to be addressed by you, a human full of empathy who wants to lead other humans full of emotions. Emotions are a given, so we as bold business leaders need to learn how to work with them. Like most hurdles, you can pick them up and use them in your battle for success if you need to.

Sales training touches on ways to do this; Stephen Covey hit it with number five of his seven habits. Let me summarize what the experts say: Let the person you are speaking with know that you heard them and that you understand them.

Take any contentious hot topic—think gun control or abortion rights. You can fundamentally disagree (or agree) with others on these topics. If you disagree, you can still hear what they say and understand their point of view. This is where you demonstrate the belief that they are an intelligent human with real-life experiences who came to their conclusion in much the same way you did. This means that you must understand their point of view, and let them know this. It does not mean you have to agree with it.

For example, take turn signal usage. I use my turn signals all of the time. Even in parking lots and when going through my neighborhood at 4 a.m. It's a habit I am happy to have. I am so astounded by people that do not use their turn signals I've had bumper stickers made that read, "Turn Signals - Not Just for Talented Drivers." Let me know if you want one.

Friends of mine feel like turn signals are a blinking nuisance that should be removed from all vehicles. Nothing frustrates them

221

more than rolling down the highway following someone with their turn signal on for miles.

We joke about their insistence on non-usage and my arguably over-usage. I wonder how they don't get hit at every four way stop they turn left at and they wonder how I don't spend every weekend replacing bulbs around my car. We may disagree, but we can still discuss the topic and move on with our lives.

One of the ways to do this from a logistical point of view is to follow these steps when you respond:

1. **Compliment:** "It's interesting that you say that."
2. **Confirm:** "<Reword what they said to clarify you heard correctly.>"
3. **Curiosity:** "Why do you suppose that is?"

You compliment the person you're speaking with on their insight. You confirm you heard what they said by repeating it back using the keywords they used. Then you add a question of curiosity to continue deepening your understanding by listening to their clarification. It flows like this:

Conversationalist: "Turn signals are a waste of time. When people do use them, they leave them on forever."

Empathic Listener: "It's interesting that you say that. When some people do use their turn signal, it seems like a challenge. Why do you suppose that is?"

Conversationalist: "Well I suppose because their attention is everywhere else but on their driving..."

Or you can go the Covey route and say, *"You feel <insert feeling> about <what you were discussing>."* Something like, *"You feel frustrated about the uselessness of turn signals."*

Here's where a challenge comes in. People aren't necessarily looking for you to fix their problems; they simply want you to listen and understand them. They want you to fulfill their emotional needs by offering your ear, nothing more.

I'm a business owner, an entrepreneur, and I fix things for a living. I imagine you do too. When people tell me to look at their flat tire, I need to be sure they don't want me to bring over the air pump. Some people just want you to admire the flat tire and feel their pain with them for a bit. It's annoying and completely escapes most logic. However, many people need that, and you and your business need many people. Like dealing with taxes, emotions are a necessary burden.

Lessons Learned: Listen Before Fixing

My wife will come home from work and detail the issues of her day. I used to attempt to fix the issues she presented. I'd offer solutions, saying things like, *"Can you do this or that?"* I have since learned to say simply, "That's too bad. You work very hard. I am sorry you have to deal with <insert issue here>." It works great, and I hate it.

You can continue the conversation by saying things like, *"Tell me more"* and *"How did that make you feel?"* Keep in mind that these are examples that emphasize the need to actually listen. Outside of the fact that someone is puking their problems all over you, they may actually mention something you want to know. Plus, it's the nice thing to do.

> **"When you start to develop your powers of empathy and imagination, the whole world opens up to you."**
> -Susan Sarandon

Communication Without Words

What you say before you actually say something is pretty important. Your website, logo, business card, and, at the top of the list, how you dress.

How do you communicate? Share it with me!

What to Wear in Business
by Krystle Marks, Personal Stylist
lovekrystle.com

What would it be like to share a glimpse of who you are and what you value without needing to say a word? How could that positively affect you and your business? It is an honor, as a personal stylist, to guide people just like you into finding their ideal work wardrobes. It mostly involves asking questions of self-discovery to get to the core of who you are. The ultimate goal is to have the gifts and talents that reside on the inside of you be communicated on the outside. Are you a creative thinker with a mind that thinks outside of the box? Do you value order and timelines? Are you the big visionary and people connector? These things can be communicated before any words are spoken.

There is one more thing I have to say before diving into this process with you. If you are an entrepreneur or a business owner, please remember this: What you present to the world matters. I am not suggesting that you need to be in a suit or even that you can't wear denim, but no matter what you choose to do, make it clean, polished, and professional. This is important stuff. Our exterior is the first communication we offer. It would be wise to give it as much thought as the car you drive or the house you buy. This is your walking advertisement. Invest in it; take it seriously. Most importantly, be free to be you and have fun with it! Here are some steps you can take to help you discover your style type and how to build a work wardrobe you enjoy wearing.

Step 1. Define

I want you to be confident in the foundation and direction you take when creating your business wardrobe. Please explore these questions:

Write down three words that best describe you.

What are your top three life values?

If we met for coffee for the first time, what would you want me to walk away knowing about you?

What style types are you drawn to? Here are some descriptions:

CLASSIC: Clean, Stripes, Polished, Preppy

ROMANTIC: Lace, Floral, Feminine

RUSTIC: Boots, Flannel, Weathered/Relaxed

URBAN: Neutral Palette, Different Textures, Fashion Forward

ROCKER: Edgy, Fun, Unexpected

BOHO CHIC: Haute Hippie, Colorful, Detailed, Earthy

GLAM: Sparkle Accents, Metallic Finishes, Neutral Palette

Step 2. Build

Now that you have defined a true reflection of you, your values, and what you want others to know about you, we can build a wardrobe that will allow you to mix and match in confidence. Here is a checklist of helpful pieces to have in your work wardrobe.

☐ *A Lean Suit (preferably neutral)*

Like I said before, a suit is not a mandatory outfit for work wardrobes. There are very few professions that require you to wear a suit for work in our current culture. However, having a two-piece suit that fits you like a glove adds immense value to your work wardrobe. Think about all the different ways you can split up and wear a well-tailored two-piece suit:

Suit pants + button-down shirt or blouse

Blazer + t-shirt + jeans
Blazer + button down shirt + chino pants
Suit pants + sweater
Blazer + Dress
Suit pants + Button down shirt + cardigan...

☐ *Chiffon Blouses and Button-Down Shirts*
You only need a few. I would suggest having one in a neutral color, one with a stripe or pattern, and one in a color. Great for layering or wearing alone.

☐ *Pull-Over Sweaters and Cardigans*
These are great layering pieces. You can wear anything from a t-shirt to a button-down underneath them or pair them with a jacket/blazer.

☐ *Jackets and Blazers*
When you wear a fitted jacket or blazer, you add an element that looks polished, put together, and well-tailored. A complete win-win.

☐ *Dresses and Skirts*
Ladies, I promise you, dresses and skirts are the most flattering pieces you will ever own. They can be dressed up or down. In the cooler months, you can wear knit tights or fleece leggings to keep your legs warm. Adding boots and jackets will keep it functional.

Step 3. Polish
This is where we change getting dressed into actually making an outfit. Adding interest with the little details makes your look feel intentional and well thought-out. These five tips will have you dressing like a pro instantly.

1. Roll - The style right now is not perfect-looking rolls. I coined the phrase "the dirty roll," which is basically just implying that you don't want it perfect. You want it to look relaxed, effortless, and little undone. What you can roll:

Denim: Roll to the ankle or just above it.

Button-down shirts or blouses: Roll 2-3 times

Sweaters with button-down shirts or blouses: These look amazing rolled together at the sleeve.

Chino pants: Roll to the ankle or just above it.

Button-down shirts or blouses with blazers and jackets: Rolled together at the sleeve. Another option is to pull the shirt sleeve down so it is exposed then roll the jacket or blazer sleeve by itself.

2. Tuck - No matter how you feel about your stomach, tucking your tops, tees, and button-downs gives you shape and creates interest. You can full tuck (all the way around) or front tuck. It might take some practice, but it's well worth mastering!

3. Layer - Any opportunity you have to layer a jacket, sweater, vest, blazer, dress, blouse... do it! Try to think outside of the box with this one, and don't be afraid to play.

4. Accessorize - Belts, watches, jewelry, scarves, bags, hats. Find what you really like and and pile it on. This is the icing on the cake when putting an outfit together.

5. Shoes - Shoes can elevate your outfit by quite a bit. They can also take your outfit down a few notches. So please pay attention to current shoes trends! If you have had shoes in your closet that are more than 5 years old, chances are it is time to consider an update. Look for minimal, non-chunky styles. And say no to square toes.

These are some of the best tricks in my magic styling hat! Enjoy the art of dressing yourself for work. Draw yourself out and shine on in confidence.

Chapter 13

Leadership and other ways to get kicked really hard.

"
*"An army of sheep led by a lion can defeat
an army of lions led by a sheep."*
-African Proverb
"

Few things in business are more necessary than a great leader. Great leaders aren't born. They are created, usually by getting the crap beat out of them through making bad decisions, overcoming challenges, and exercising a stubborn will.

When I first started my business, I was doing everything I was supposed to "to get things in order." I was designing a logo, a website, business cards, setting up a telephone, organizing my office, and creating a plan for marketing and inventory. I was reading books and taking classes on all-things-business—i's dotted and t's crossed. It was a big beautiful jigsaw puzzle, and everything seemed to fit where it was supposed to.

I remember perusing a list of business courses at our local

university's small-business development center. I saw classes on taxes and accounting, marketing, and employees and human resource issues.

I acknowledged that taxes and accounting and marketing were big deals. Employee-management classes? Meh. Those seemed futile at best. I was pretty sure I just needed to hire a person or two, pay them some cash, and they'd do their jobs with no questions asked and no baggage of any kind.

That was one of the most foolish assumptions I've ever made. The problem with human resources is that they are, at their core, humans. And to err is human. So I was hiring people who were destined to make mistakes.

It turns out that I have a powerful work ethic. I was raised to work my knuckles to the bone, to show up on time, to do what's asked of me, and to do it with a smile. I aim to do these tasks even better than expected, not to complain, and to get the job done. I used to assume that everyone had a work ethic like this. Why wouldn't they?

My perspective changed when I hired my first employee. I was amazed at how oddly incapable a human can be at things so simple. Where did I mess up? I wondered at this because, as dumb as this first hire was, I had to admit I was the leader who hired him. So who was at fault? Me.

Some people are made to work for other people because without leaders like you and me, they'd be challenged to remember to exhale after they inhale. I'm not so sure how they made it as far as they did. When I interview them for a job I'd pay them for, I'm left wondering where our society has gone awry.

 Lessons Learned: Be a Great Leader

Leadership is tough. That's why great leaders are held in such high regard in history books. It's necessary to become a great leader to grow your bold business.

Who's Awesome?

After a dazzling array of interview questions and an enormous roster of bad hires, I finally settled on a system for interviewing that works for my businesses. As you consider my approach, remember that this process probably needs to be tweaked for your exact business.

My secrets for interviews that lead to solid hires:

1. **Read body and facial language** more than the verbal answers of your interviewee. This includes watching eye movements to give cues that the interviewee may be lying, as well as looking for simple things such as the appearance of engagement (crossed arms vs. hands on table). Check out the book *What Every Body is Saying* by Joe Navarro for much more information on this fascinating topic.

2. **Ask unexpected questions.** Questions like "What is your biggest weakness?" are not allowed. Instead use questions like, "If your friends were talking about you behind your back, what would they make fun of you for?" Get the potential employee's mind working much harder to give you an honest answer.

3. **Start the interview off as if you're going to hire them.** Let the interview either fill you with regret over your choice or confirm that you made a fine decision.

4. **No projects.** You don't have the time to "fix" people. All people come with baggage. Make sure they can leave it at the door.

5. **Forget about school grades.** How were your grades in school? This doesn't mean you don't want a smart employee, but book smarts may not be what you need. Have a way to test the intelligence and skills for the specific tasks you need the employee to accomplish.

6. **Create a real-life-like scenario** for the interviewee to prove themselves fit for the task.

231

Lessons Learned: Unexpected Interviews Can Break Potential Weak Hires

I was having a hard time finding smart, caring, charismatic, and mechanically inclined printer repair service technicians. I knew that service with a smile was 80% of our job. The actual repair was 20%. So if the charisma was not there, the interview was short. If the interviewee did have the charisma we were looking for, we had them look at a printer to diagnose a jam issue.

The problematic printer to diagnose would jam at the same spot every time: next to a roller that had a small, yellow electrical wire disconnected from a plug inside the printer, not more than an inch from the jammed paper. We would give the interviewee 5 minutes to find the problem or at least describe the possible issues.

I have to admit that it was entertaining to watch the reaction of interviewees who could, as they assured me, "fix anything," when I reached in and plugged in the blatantly obvious wire they missed. Whether it was nerves or frustration, more than a couple interviewees struggled longer to produce excuses than they did to attempt a diagnosis.

The idea was not to have them solve the issue, but to witness the diagnostic process. Red faces at customer sites does not a confident customer make. Excuses for not accomplishing a task are even worse.

Of course, after you hire your potential golden hire, you'll need to train them. And you'll still have to find out what baggage they failed to inform you of during the interview: "That nice car I drove here? Yeah, that's my brother's." "I don't really know how to work email. It's just one of those things." "You want me to show up every single weekday?"

I've heard all of these and more. Nothing is as entertaining as listening to excuses from employees... until you realize you're paying them. If you've ever hired an employee, your list of odd statements may even be superior to mine.

Employees have baggage and can be a brutal pain. But still, I've often wondered why some business owners swear off employees. I was speaking with a plumber who told me "never again." That means that he'd rather risk the livelihood that provides for his family than to deal with employees. That speaks volumes on management, business, and the state of work ethic in our society.

In the end, I believe that this particular plumber (and most small business owners) who swear off employees are doing themselves a disservice. Employees are like a colonoscopy. They are a necessary pain in the ass.

Sure, employees want time off, higher pay, and more benefits, and that's not to mention the constant barrage of political and legal issues concerning human resource regulations. But employees are a multiplier, and you need multipliers to make it as a bold business owner. (See Chapter 11 for more on multipliers.)

Bold business owners like you have employees do tasks and jobs that either you don't want to do or are unable to do, even if the reason you're unable to do them is you being on vacation. Well, especially if the reason you're unable to do that job is being on vacation.

Do you know how many business owners forego vacation because they are reportedly too busy? The answer is too many.

Now let's talk about actually utilizing employees. First stop: deciding you need help. I don't mean help like from a psychiatrist or doctor. I mean you have a lot of stuff to do and need help getting it all done.

Have a great employee story?
Share it with me!

> *"Always treat your employees exactly as you want them to treat your best customers."*
> -Stephen R. Covey

To Err is Employee

The first and most major lesson most new employers learn is that all employees are human. Humans have needs, wants, dreams, and desires, which they hope, on some level, working for you can fulfill. Your job as a leader is to do your best to fulfill those needs and wants as best you can in exchange for these employees doing their absolute best for you.

This should be stated during the interview. Your company culture should also be mentioned. Every company has a culture, some strict and unpleasant, others more lively and free. Often, a company with a lively and free company culture can get away with paying less in exchange for increased freedom. Rigid company cultures are typically undesired.

> *"95 percent of my assets drive out of the gate every evening. It's my job to maintain a work environment that keeps those people coming back every morning."*
> -Jim Goodnight CEO of SAS

When employees, subcontractors, and other multipliers are introduced into your business, that makes you a leader. Ready or not.

How many jobs have you had that allowed people in authoritative positions to discredit and disregard the employees under them? This typically leads to a lowering of employee morale, which leads to employees leaving. So don't be this kind of leader. There are simply too many jobs available for good employees.

Bad employees will usually have a challenge finding a job. Truly good employees are a rare commodity. That's why leadership and company culture are so important. Talk to just about any business owner and you'll either hear how employees are their downfall or the greatest thing since getting paid cash.

> **"Train people well enough so they can leave, treat them well enough so they don't want to."**
>
> Richard Branson

Really?

I once hired an employee that seemed too good to be true. I knew I was selling my business and thought, "Wherever I go, I am taking this kid with me." He was phenomenal. He was super social, clients loved him, and he seemed to be able to do the jobs at hand with ease.

One day I received a phone call from a client that led me down a rabbit-hole of discovering dropped balls and gargantuan failures. This employee ended up costing me over $15,000 in less than a month by misrepresenting repairs and telling customers outrageous lies. The story gets pretty deep, so let's just say I made a hiring error.

When I called all the clients that we had failed and explained the situation to them, my $15,000 issue suddenly seemed like nothing. Most of my clients had employee horror stories that topped that number by many thousands of dollars.

 Lessons Learned: Employees Can Cause Headaches

What I mean to say with this chapter is to use employees as a multiplier. Just be aware that they can be one of your biggest headaches. Get your hiring systems, as well as the systems you want your employees to implement, in place before you hire.

Leadership is More

One of the things that separate leaders from managers is that true leaders command respect and trust just about anywhere they go. They do this by helping anyone they can. I do everything in my power to introduce and connect people from my network to each other. I don't get anything directly from it other than the feeling that I am helping someone. That's good enough for me. (See Chapter 12 section: Work Harder to Introduce Than to be Introduced).

Eventually, you hope, all of this help will work its way back to you in the form of more clients of a higher caliber. I recommend that bold business owners skip this desire and just connect people. Simply make the world a better place.

> *"I stand here before you not as a prophet, but as a humble servant of you, the people."*
> -Nelson Mandela

My advice to help others by connecting them with others is simply to illustrate how leadership goes beyond your business. It should carry over into your everyday life. Open doors for people, chat with others while waiting in line, always have a compliment for someone, and treat everyone you meet with respect, even the people you're less than fond of. Your job as a great leader is to get others to follow you.

As a business person who owns a company that deals with phone companies, I can assure you that trying times will come. Tech support that is not technically supportive will be tough to tolerate. Your business will need to overcome obstacles that challenge your resolve. However, the payoff is an increase is leadership skills.

Everyone has their limitations, I understand. Your job is to keep in mind the cost of breaking from your bold business code of conduct. Let your success be the shot heard 'round the world.

> *"The challenge of leadership is to be strong, but not rude; be kind, but not weak; be bold, but not a bully; be thoughtful, but not lazy; be humble, but not timid; be proud, but not arrogant; have humor, but without folly."*
>
> -Jim Rohn

Chapter 14

Service begins when you serve.

" "

"Nobody raves about average."

-Bill Quiseng

What is the most important trait for a service employee? Many people would answer this question quickly, claiming that the skillset is the most important. Another group of intelligent people would claim that loyalty to the business is so tough to come by that it must be the most important. The true answer, in my experience, has been the ability to communicate is the most important trait for a service employee.

My first clue was that you and I are consumers first. Even without owning a business, we need service employees. You can't help but interact with them. Stuff breaks, whether it's a broken appliance or a broken car. Sometimes that stuff needs to be repaired by a professional.

Think of the last time the cable guy showed up at your

house or the last time you had your furnace checked out. Were you excited to deal with those issues? How did you feel about the service professional who resolved your issue?

Service professionals often destroy their own chances of growing their business by failing in the realm of communication. Let's clarify what a customer wants and what a service professional can offer.

We can agree on a few things. First, let's assume that every service professional has the minimum qualification to fix your problem. The person coming to fix your refrigerator has some knowledge of what they'll need to do to repair it. Secondly, this service professional will need the tools to actually perform the task. What good is knowledge without the tools to utilize that knowledge, right? Finally, the service professional will need to have a company that stands behind the work. Maybe it's a one-person company or maybe it is a huge franchise that offers systems and logos and all the good stuff for the technicians. Unless you are having your unemployed cousin turn some screws on your broken item, it's assumed that the company has hired employees who know how to fix your stuff and have the tools to do it.

Let's also assume that 98% of all the professionals you call to service and repair your stuff have these three things. The difference between them will come down to communication. To truly explain this stance, I need to list the modes of communication included. In this sense, communication will be represented by all forms including verbal, visual, auditory as well as marketing and the customer's perception of your company. To keep up with this train of thought, let's consider two scenarios:

Scenario #1

Your sink is broken and you need a plumber. You go to the internet and find one. You call the company and get a voicemail, so you try a few more companies. After four or five attempts, you finally reach a plumber. The phone is answered with a gruff "Yeah?" to which you respond by asking for clarification and learn

239

that this is, in fact, a plumbing company and that this person can, in fact, send a plumber to fix your sink. They set up a time for them to visit your house "sometime tomorrow."

You take a day off work, wait until 4:17 p.m., call the plumbing company, and voicemail answers. You call again at 4:49 p.m. and notice a rusty white van pulling into your driveway. You think it's the plumber, but see no markings on the van to confirm it. You hang up the phone as the voicemail message fires up again.

A chubby, unshaven guy with his shirt half untucked walks up your sidewalk and bangs on the door as if he is trying to punch it down. You answer the door, he moves past you with barely a hello, and asks where the problem sink is.

As you show him the issue, he bends down to start working away while you are still describing the problem. He smells like a combination of cigarettes, burritos, and a very new and semi-repulsive car air freshener. He seems to be coughing a lot, as if he has some snot wad in his throat that refuses to budge. You back up and mention to him that you will leave him to his work. He grunts and bends over, showing you his backside, crack and all. His pants are stained and his shirt has some tears in it. It only gets better, as you can imagine.

Does your sink get fixed? Yes. Are you happy? Sort of. Would you recommend them to your friends? Only you can answer that.

Scenario #2:

Your sink is broken and you need a plumber. You go to the internet and find one. You call this company and get one of the gentlest, kindest voices you have ever heard. The voice asks you questions about your problem and clarifies a few details. After a short and sweet conversation, you're given the option of having a plumber out today at a certain cost or a plumber out tomorrow at a lower cost. You love your sink, so you request today. The reassuring voice on the other end explains that a plumber will be to your address in less than two hours.

Forty-five minutes later, a beautiful van with a dazzling logo appears in your driveway. Out pops a smiling, fit, professional plumber. He rings your doorbell, waits for you to answer, and offers a kind greeting. The plumber asks for permission to enter your home.

You lead him to the problematic sink and explain the issue. The plumber listens intently and asks you a couple easy, relevant questions. You answer and leave the plumber to his work.

He happens to be wearing a clean, tucked-in shirt with his name and the company logo embroidered on it. He smells nice and speaks confidently and to your level, nothing too technical. He uses his neatly ordered tools to repair your sink. It only gets better, as you can imagine.

Does your sink get fixed? Yes. Are you happy? Yes. Would you recommend them to your friends? Only you can answer that.

Customer Preferences

So we have a few problems in both scenarios. First, how do you know what type of plumber you are going to get? Online reviews are one possibility. Referrals from friends are another. The real truth is that so many service companies provide service like that in Scenario #1 that people do not expect Scenario #2. It's a pipe dream, especially when it comes to plumbers.

So when faced with Scenario #2, how does the customer feel? The customer trusts your company and the technician. Do you want to see how much of a difference communication can make? Let's take Scenario #1 and assume the service professional is the best plumber the world has ever seen. Let's say Scenario #2 has literally the worst plumber who still has a job in the plumbing industry. Which would you rather have working on your sink? The point, of course, is that communication plays a huge factor, if it's not THE factor, in a customer's decision to use your services.

In this example, even the worst plumber in the world should be able to repair a sink. The law of diminishing returns in regards to skillset is definitely part of the equation.

Let's look at this from a different angle. Imagine how much more it costs the plumbing company in Scenario #2 versus the company in Scenario #1. Is there really that much more of a cost to adjusting these few things? A clean truck or van, clean clothes, and a respectful technician can make all the difference.

We should take this a step further and ask how much more the plumber in Scenario #2 could charge over what the plumber in Scenario #1 charges? Would it surprise you if I told you that you can typically charge four times what others in your industry charge for excellent service?

> **"My theory is that if you look confident, you can pull off anything. Even if you have no clue what you're doing."**
>
> -Jessica Alba

Before you jump out of your seat and cry foul, let me defend the claim, then you can decide if this option fits your company.

Scenario #1 plumber clearly has a lack mentality. He doesn't hold much in high esteem. For whatever reason, this plumber is stuck in the deep well of believing that he can be the cheapest and all will be OK. He's probably charging less than he should in the first place. Let's say, for example, that he is charging $50 an hour. The average hourly rate around his local service area is probably double that. But he did a bit of research and decided he would be the cheapest to get more business. Not a terrible idea, at first. At least until you explore the other options.

By my 4x rule, Scenario #2 plumber can then charge $200 an hour. That's a pretty hefty sum at this point for a plumber, would you agree? But is it worth the cost?

To answer this question, we need to look at the communication once again. When you called the plumber in Scenario #1, you were lucky to get through to a human. You caught a grouch that answered the phone. So, your expectations for what success looks like in your head went from a great plumber, to a good plumber, to just a plumber that is available, to any human being. All of this happened over the course of a few minutes as your frustration with the world of plumbers rose.

When you called the plumber in Scenario #2, you were still at wanting a great plumber. If you hadn't called them until your third or fourth attempt to reach a plumber, you would have jumped at $200. You have reached a human who is nice and can solve your problem.

This is the pricing dance. Service, quality, and price have been labeled as the three distinct differences between companies. Offer great service and quality and you can command a higher price. If you lower your quality and service, you have to lower your prices to survive.

It's unrealistic to offer the best quality and service and still have the lowest price. Why would you want to? Quality and service cost money for you to implement. The difference is that the cost of implementing higher quality and service is a fraction of what you can charge for your service. Overall, I believe it's worth the cost.

In addition, you have the pride of your business to stand by. Can you imagine being the plumber in Scenario #1 and telling your friends you have your own business? Would they congratulate you to your face and roll their eyes behind your back?

Scenario #2 plumber also works for a company that is much more marketable. It will sell for more money to a qualified buyer because of a wonderful reputation and a beautiful product. In this case, the product is a plumbing business. Anybody can start a crappy company with rusty trucks and disgruntled employees.

> *"Nobody cares how much you know, until they know how much you care."*
> -Theodore Roosevelt

Lessons Learned: People Crave Trust

Your potential clients have to deal with a chaotic world. If you offer them a real reason to trust you (something along the lines of you are kind and do what you say you will) then your clients will spread the word about your awesomeness for miles around. Great communication is so rare that any company that even attempts a bit of customer service gets flooded with praise.

Let's break down some costs for these two scenarios, to put things into perspective. This perspective will rely on the 80/20 rule, as many things in business do. You will gain 80% more profit by tweaking your business 20%.

We are going to convert Scenario #1 plumber into Scenario #2 plumber. What will we need:

-Receptionist/Dispatch company or employee (full time with backup)

-Nice truck/van

-Nice clothes

-Customer-service trained techs

- Nice toolbox and tools

The most expensive portion of this makeover is going to be the addition of either an employee or a receptionist service to answer your incoming phone calls. If you use a service, I would recommend a vendor that allows you to have a trained receptionist of your own, such as Calls On Call (www.callsoncall.com).

Your other option is to hire a full-time receptionist or two part-time receptionists. Depending on the volume of calls you receive, a service like Calls On Call will run anywhere from a few hundred dollars to several hundred dollars per month. A full-time receptionist will cost you around $2500-3500+ per month.

The nice van will run you perhaps $20,000 more than a rusty but trusty(ish) kidnapping van. This includes the vinyl wrap that makes the van a rolling billboard for your company. Note:

Spray painted windows don't shout out, "Trust me!"

The clothes will cost you a few hundred dollars a year. You can either purchase the clothes outright or use a service to provide and launder them. Regardless of how you do it, the costs are pretty reasonable.

Customer service training can run anywhere from a few hundred dollars for a one-time thing to a few thousand dollars for routine training. I recommend routine training to keep the value of customer service top of mind.

Every plumber needs tools. A toolbox and the routine cleaning of a service professional's tools are really the only tool costs on the company's end. So let's estimate this to be a few hundred dollars a year.

So if we add up all of these numbers and look at them annually, we have an estimate of around $40,000 at the high end. This presumes you pay $20,000 per year for a van. The low estimate will be around $10,000 for these changes, presuming you found a nice used van and took advantage of a service like Calls On Call.

Assuming you can charge four times more than Scenario #1 plumber, at $200 per hour you have a difference of $150 per hour. Calculating all of this, you need to sell 267 more hours annually to make up that $40K. If you go cheap and run the $10,000 option, you only need to sell 67 more hours. How big of a deal is that? It essentially breaks down to selling four to five more billable hours per week to break even at first.

Keep in mind that everything over that four to five hours per week is pure profit. That means if you were to sell two additional hours per working day, you would pocket an additional $39,000. Do this the $10K way and you pocket an additional $67,000 every year.

It gets better, as you probably know, since you have some static costs in this calculation. Let's presume you have only five incoming phone calls a day, and two of them are for paying jobs. This is a pricey endeavor, a risk, if you will. If your company in

Scenario #1 only answers half of their calls, you would likely only get one out of the two paying jobs. Because your company is not answering every call, you are not getting those two jobs. So the plumber is maybe getting one new job a day.

Let's see what happens when you answer all five of those calls. You can be assured to get those two additional jobs per day. But we still need more service calls to justify the expense. That comes with time through referrals and marketing with your neatly lettered van or truck. When you treat your business with respect, your business will grow. More calls will come in. Soon you will be up to 10 or 20 calls per day. These 20 calls will offer more opportunities for customers. The multiplier keeps adjusting what is available for you to serve.

Charging a low hourly rate for your services promises you one thing: stagnation. You will not be able to afford to grow, have access to cash, retain good employees, or get better training. You will rely on being acceptable and hit a plateau in business. Many service professionals are OK with this. They do decent work, they make OK money, and they can claim to be entrepreneurs. Yay for the mundane!

But you didn't pick up this bold business book to plateau, did you? You want to be bold. I bet you are the business owner that wants to be bolder than you already are. You need a little kick in the shorts to accentuate that boldness you carry around so humbly. Perhaps too humbly. The power to grow your business is in your hands.

> " " *"I do things my way and I pay a high price."* -John Mellencamp " "

But What If...

I want to back up a step and take a look at the bigger picture. Many service professionals had a rough time a few years ago. The economy wasn't doing so well, and many companies were folding or shrinking. Imagine you were the plumber in Scenario #1. Would you still have a job in a shrinking economy? Probably not. You'd be laid off with the rest of your co-workers due to a lack of cash flow. Your employer could not sustain the economic downturn.

Now let's imagine you are the plumber in Scenario #2. Would you still have a job? My guess is that you would. Plumbers will always have the potential for work. Do you think the economy will get so bad that people will stop using running water? If it ever gets to that point, we have other problems.

The plumber in Scenario #2 will be more trusted, will be more accessible, be referred more often, and have the cash flow to survive bumps in the economy. The plumbing company in Scenario #2 understands business. The plumbing company in Scenario #1 may not understand business yet, and it could cost its employees their livelihood.

You could argue that the plumber in Scenario #1 could go off on his own, charge $50 an hour and survive. But like most things in business, I would like to challenge that notion.

As a business owner, you need to know the cost of doing business. If you have a service business, you want to know the cost of having an employee go out the door and perform a service. Even if that employee goes down the road three blocks and is at the customer's site for five minutes, there are costs involved. When I calculated this cost for my printer repair business, it was right around $52. Every time a trained technician got into a car and drove somewhere, there was a cost of at least $52. Take a moment and calculate your costs. They may surprise you.

The opportunity cost alone is worth exploring just to make the point. If you have one job for your technician that takes all day and you charge $60 per hour, you will get $480 of revenue for that work. You will pay out about $200 of that to the tech and in taxes. Perhaps you pay a bit more, depending on your employee's benefit package. Then you have a vehicle, training, tools, a building, utilities, marketing and advertising, clothes, software, other vendors such as accountants, snow removal and lawn care, security, your time, and the money you want to earn.

How can you earn enough cash doing things this way to grow your business or to fund the life you dream about? The truth is that you simply cannot. Should we take it a step further? This is The Bold Business Book, not the Suckers Philosophy on Survival Book, so let's push.

⬥ Lessons Learned: Commit to Growth

My recommendation to anyone in business is to grow your business as if you were preparing to sell it or give it to your child. No one is likely to buy a defunct business, and gifting a struggling business to your children is just mean. Keep this rule in mind and your business decisions will be much easier.

The Value of Money

I want to be clear in this description. In a few years, these figures will probably be laughable. Inflation is a thing, right?

I had a seminar attendee mention that she was frustrated with the high cost of things. Basically, inflation did not alter the value of a dollar in her mind. Stuff around her continued to get more expensive while she maintained her price point. She felt that it was her place to slow inflation by charging $40 per hour for her services. In her mind, her one-person, 20-client practice was going to alter the fate of the world economy over the course of a few months. That isn't going to happen.

I told her to raise her prices by a factor of three. She gasped in disbelief, until the audience backed me up and said she was crazy for not charging what she was worth.

Chapter 15

The business stuff other books don't teach you.

"
"

"Play the game."

-My dad

This is chapter is why you grabbed this book. We are going to cover a bunch of tidbits to run your business smoothly; the stuff that business schools just don't teach. These things combined may save you so much time you just might be able to surf the web without any guilt of wasted time. Maybe...

Tidbit 1: Meetings

Have you ever been in a meeting that seemed to go on way too long? I've been in meetings that were scheduled for an hour, and the attendees got what they needed to get done in 20 minutes. Then they desperately tried to extend the meeting to fill that hour.

Attendee 1: "Well that about wraps it up. Thanks for meeting with me."

Attendee 2: "Since I have you here, would you mind helping me solve world hunger really quick?"

Typically, attendees are too polite to stand up and say, "That sounds like a great topic to add onto the agenda at a later date." In most instances, I recommend that you be the attendee who stands up and lets everyone know that you have another commitment or some other reason to get out of there. Why waste your time on meetings that aren't productive?

 Lessons Learned: There Will Always be People Willing to Waste Your Time.

Meetings are the black hole of progress. Meetings often become babble sessions with no real progress outside of a few choice minutes where the real collaboration happened. Sure, meetings have their place in regard to business etiquette in a social setting. Outside of that, keep track of the value of your meeting time.

If you're not going into a meeting with an agenda, you need to ask yourself what you hope to accomplish. What is your personal agenda? Do you know the agendas of the other attendees? As with most things in business, having a system will save you time, make you look more organized and professional, and help with your overall time management and success.

The system I suggest for business meetings is easy:
1. Schedule the meeting.
2. Verify the appointment 24 hours before meeting.
3. Have an agenda.
4. Share the agenda.
5. Get LOTS of stuff done.

6. Set and verify CLEAR NEXT STEPS for participants.
7. Follow-up with meeting participants.
8. Thank meeting participants.

You'll notice some redundancy. If we set a meeting, why do we need to verify the meeting? There is a rule that I've discovered in business that defines why we need verification and follow-up. The rule is people forget stuff, so it helps to remind them.

People have more going on than a meeting with you. You need to remind people of the meeting as well as why you are meeting. Meetings can be very productive if everyone has a clear agenda that has been shared. Without these reminders, you will find yourself alone in a conference room because a date was mixed up or a time was miscommunicated. Alone in a conference room is a terrible place to be. Because then you need to play the game of, who messed up.

Lessons Learned: Many People Do Not Advance in Organizations or Care Past 8th Grade

My wife teaches 8th grade. I run a few businesses. We come home with the same stories. They typically go like this: "This guy shows up late most of the time, and when he eventually shows up, he just plays on his phone. When he doesn't play on his phone, he leaves for a few minutes. I have no idea where he goes." Does that sound like a challenging 8th grader? Believe it or not, I was talking about a 50-year-old lawyer in a business group I belong to.

It may be worth noting that, every once in awhile, you're going to be the 8th grader and people will roll their eyes at you. You'll forget about a meeting or run late. You'll be waiting for that one important call during your meeting. If you find yourself behaving this way, understand that your actions reflect on your reputation. Be in the moment doing what you told people you would do.

Make sure you do all that you can so that you are living your life anticipating, rather than reacting. You can anticipate traffic, emails, etc. Reacting to them will frustrate you and the people you are supposed to meet with. No one's life needs to be that hectic.

If you're on time for your meetings, keep the meeting flowing well, accomplish a lot, follow up, and you will be golden. People will appreciate you because it will be crystal clear that you appreciate them. The downside, of course, is that you will be invited to other meetings. This brings us to our next tidbit that you need to know.

> *"One look at an email can rob you of 15 minutes of focus. One call on your cell phone, one tweet, one instant message can destroy your schedule, forcing you to move meetings, or blow off really important things, like love, and friendship.."*
>
> -Jacqueline Leo

Tidbit 2: The Power of No

Never underestimate the power of no. When I started my business, I said yes all the time—yes to clients, yes to friends, yes to vendors, yes to family, yes to charities, yes to advertisers. I was a yes man to the world. Do you know where this was leading me? To no-man's land. I was basically in a desert with a lot of stuff to do and not enough time or money to do it. I was overcommitted and had little to show for it, save for a very long to-do list. If you do this, you'll also have a list of people who you believe will be exceedingly annoyed if you don't satisfy their expectations. If you're doing this, stop and rethink your strategy.

When someone comes to you asking for your help, you need to ask a few simple questions:

252

1. What will happen if I decide not to do this?
2. Will it hurt our relationship?
3. Will I enjoy this?
4. Will the world be better if I do this?
5. Will the world be measurably better or just idealistically?
6. Let's say I help this person now. What if in three years, I desperately need this person's help. Will this person be willing to drop everything to help me? If the answer is no, you have your answer as well.
7. What is the opportunity cost of doing or not doing this?

This may seem like an awful lot of questions to run through when someone asks for help, but in some cases, it's necessary. A much simpler way may be to simply ask yourself, "What will happen if I say no?" You'll be surprised how often the answer is nothing. No fallout at all. Not a big deal. Just don't do it, end of story.

Keep in mind the cost of the question for the favor-asker vs. the cost of the answer for you. For example, someone could ask you, "Hey, would you mind being on the committee for saving the mosquitos?" The cost of that question is about three seconds of time. That's it. If you say no, the asker will move along to the next victim. The asker may attempt to talk you into joining after your initial no. So let's say they have a few minutes of time invested in asking you. I will call that very low risk. But suppose you say yes to the request. You just committed to monthly meetings, fundraising, and talking up this meeting to your colleagues. Actual cost of the answer to you: 12 years of wasted time. I'd call that extremely high risk. What else could you do with that time?

I should also mention that the power of no will lose some power if you're not nice about it. If you just literally use the one-word answer, you may turn off the requestor. The requestor may be able to help you in business or refer you at some point in the future. Perhaps they're already a client. In addition, as we discussed before, people have emotions that need to be coddled. Instead of just saying no, use something that is a little softer, such as, "I sincerely appreciate the offer, and I am happy that you thought of me for this. However, due to the tight schedule I already have, I feel like I would not be able to devote as much time to this cause as it deserves." This is how people like to be told no. To break that down for you, it goes like this:

1. I sincerely appreciate the offer
2. Compliment or flattering statement
3. However, (do NOT use the word "but") due to *<insert unsolvable issue here>.*
4. I feel like I would not be able to *<insert undesired result that prevents you from saying yes>.*

Can you imagine dating going like this? Well, actually it does (for some people).

Requestor: "Will you go out with me?"
Deny-er: "I sincerely appreciate you asking, and I am so impressed that you came over here to ask me. However, due to the tight schedule, I feel like I wouldn't be able to devote as much time to you as you deserve."

Others just say no and roll their eyes, in my experience anyway.

Tidbit 3: Opportunity costs are often very high.

Every time you spend time or money on something, you have an opportunity cost. Opportunity cost can come in the form of time, money, or effort. For example, if you own a house that has a mortgage, you are paying interest on your mortgage. Suppose you have an annual interest rate of 5% and a loan amount of $300,000. Every year you are paying about $15,000 in interest. This means that every dollar you spend on anything other than your mortgage costs you 5 cents. So that $1 candy bar is really costing you $1.05. (And it adds an inch to your thighs.) Over 30 years that candy bar actually cost you 150% more than retail!

If you buy something you don't need for $5000, it's costing you an extra $250, annually. If you've got a 30-year mortgage, that $5000 boat that you never use will end up costing you 150% more than retail as well. Or $12,500, presuming you paid cash for the boat.

Lessons Learned: Borrow a Boat

Seriously, unless you play with it every weekend, a boat is a money pit. Tons of your friends probably already have boats. Use theirs. Or rent a boat. Do you know why they don't have aquatic vehicle investment funds? It's tough to win the money game with a boat.

My point isn't not to have any fun or buy candy bars. You must simply be aware of the cost of the fun you choose, so that you can choose wisely. I'll illustrate this with a motorcycle I once purchased for a few thousand dollars. I rode it quite a bit the first year. For the next 12 years, my motorcycle riding decreased straight down to less than 100 miles per year. With maintenance costs, the actual cost per mile to ride was around $6. Including the value of the bike, keeping it was costing me hundreds of dollars every year, plus valuable garage space. Having the ability to jump on the motorcycle and feel the open road, something I rarely did, was costing me a lot of money. So I took a picture of the bike and sold it.

Opportunity cost can come in the form of time as well. The opportunity cost of time is much more valuable than money. Money will come and go. Time is limited. A great way to determine opportunity cost is the rocking chair test.

The rocking chair test is simple. Pretend you are 90-years-old and sitting in a rocking chair on your porch. You're thinking about all that you have done and accomplished in your life. Now think about a decision you're going to make today. How does the projected result make you feel? Are you happy you decided a certain way? Does it even matter when you are 90?

A great example of the rocking chair test is to imagine sitting in a plane, about to jump out, with a parachute. If you decide not to jump and go back down with the plane and land, you'll have a terrible story about how you chickened out. If you just go ahead and jump and feel the thrill of jumping out of a plane, your 90-year-old self will crack a smile.

How about you use the rocking chair test to decide if you want to start your own business. Or hire an employee. Or fire an employee. How will your life be different from these decisions? Will it be better?

Everything has a cost to it. That cost is not always as simple as looking at the price tag or the time estimate. What else could you do with what you would spend on this item or service? You may be surprised at the answer.

Tidbit 4: Commit to yourself.

A friend recently started his own business. He was dabbling at best and struggling a bit to stay afloat. Then someone told him he couldn't run a successful business. This naysayer told my friend that if he could, he would have already. Suddenly my friend found the drive to be committed to his business. The drive came in the form of proving some random person wrong. That was all it took. His business today is leaps and bounds beyond what even he thought it could be.

Lessons Learned: Commitment Feeds Good Decisions

Commitment means staying loyal to your decision long after the mood you were in when you decided is gone.

Commitment is the name of the game in business. In decision-making, commitment will save you. The typical credo goes something like this: decide, commit, act, then succeed. It's a simple motto that pays huge dividends. When you commit to someone or something, you decide that they are important enough to justify their cost to you. Without this commitment, your decisions are a house of cards, able to be toppled by the tiniest hint of new or different.

Can you imagine trying to start a business and not being fully committed? I run into countless people who have a business that is only being taken care of in a non-committal way. I actually heard this from one potential client: "I'll do something with my business someday." What are the chances that this business will last very long or grow to be successful?

> "Commitment is what transforms a promise into reality."
> -Abraham Lincoln

Imagine what you could do if you realized that the opportunity cost of starting your own business was too great. Imagine that you said no and committed to staying in your job. You would be like most other people in this world. Is that who you want to be? Probably not. So let's organize that question a little more appropriately.

Imagine what you could do if you realized that the opportunity cost of starting your own business was high, but the risk was worth it. Imagine you said no to your current job and committed to starting and growing your own business. Do you know what you could do with that? Almost anything you want! Commitment will lead to persistence which will lead to success.

Tidbit 5: Business is measured in time, money, and effort.

Time and money are easy to measure. That third item, effort, is a little tougher. Because of this, some people fail to measure it accurately, if at all.

For example, if you need to go to the doctor, you have an expense in time, money, and effort. You may have to pay directly or have health insurance cover the costs for you. You need time to get to the doctor, wait for the doctor, and actually be in the room with the doctor. The effort is worth exploring: How sick do you need to be to go to the doctor? A little sniffle? Or do you need to be bleeding out of at least five holes before you consider going to the doctor? The difference is effort. Perceived effort is measured by the individual, which is what makes putting a metric on the cost so difficult. A dollar is equal to a dollar and a minute is a minute. But perceptions of effort don't match up so easily. Your idea of a struggle may be someone else's idea of an easy way.

To illustrate this, let's look at running for fun. Many people think that running is meant for zombie apocalypses alone. Others feel that running is a way to clear their mind and get the blood flowing for health and wellness. So if I ask zombie runner to run a mile with no zombies in sight, they will probably give me a resounding no. If, on the other hand, I ask the health and wellness runners, they're likely to invite me to join so both of us could enjoy the pleasure of running. The zombie runner sees no pleasure in running. Running costs the same and takes about the same time. It is the perceived effort that makes all the difference.

> "There is but one degree of commitment; total."
> -Arnie Sherr

This brings us back to consider perceptions again. The beautiful thing is that you can change your perception in an instant. The zombie runner? He can become a marathon runner by committing to changing his perception to believe that running will help clear his mind and offer him better health and wellness. This change can be made in an instant.

Tidbit 6: Money and time are like blood in an ocean of sharks.

In this analogy, the sharks want to spend your money on advertising and charity, among other things. If you're making money or you have extra time, you become a tool that others wish to use. There is nothing wrong with having lots of money and time. After all, these are the end goals. You simply need to be aware that extra money and time will often give off a meaty scent in this ocean. Keep the sharks at bay with defined parameters of where you will spend your money and time.

> "*Money often costs too much.*"
> -Ralph Waldo Emerson

I once received a call from a credit card processing company. Luckily for the sales woman, she caught me at a time when I was actually considering changing providers. When I told her how much I received in monthly credit card transactions, she hung up on me. Yep, a telemarketer hung up on me. Does that even happen? Yes, I found out, it does. This telemarketer was only interested in my money (no big surprise there). The real kicker was she was interested only in my money as long as it hit a certain threshold. For a moment, I let a telemarketer make me feel inadequate. Thankfully, that feeling passed awfully fast.

I believe a well-run small company can become a well-run big company. So if you say no to small companies, you're risking future payouts and tarnishing a reputation.

Tidbit 7: Don't hate, chase, or wish evil on anyone.

You will find that as you become successful, others may try to spread negativity, often rooted in some personal emotional issue, to you. Call it jealousy if you want.

I once received a nasty-gram email from another local

small business owner because my company had tried to hire his administrative assistant. If your employees are getting job offers from other companies, that's great news. My employees get job offers all the time, often by clients. In fact, something is wrong if they don't get any. If no one wants one of my employees, something is wrong with my employee or my training.

My point is that some people find ways to spread negativity. I used to think I had to defend myself or respond in kind. But it's not worth dealing with people like that. Not by pushing back, at least. I like to use negativity judo. Which is to use their own force to help them fall in the direction they are attacking. In this case I simply asked if he would prefer that he have employees that no one else wanted?

Don't let hate of this nature alter your life. It can consume you if you're not careful. Though it is fun to listen to haters stumble over their words.

Tidbit 8: The biggest pain-in-the-ass (PIA) clients are often the smallest.

When you first start your business, you're still figuring out what works and what doesn't. This includes working with clients of all sizes and types. From my experience, it's the smallest clients that are often the biggest pain in the ass. This is not a universal rule. Clients of all sizes can be a pain. Some are just needier than others. But you'll need to decide if you want to keep working with those PIA clients. Is the headache they bring to the company worth it? Often, the answer is no. If you decide they are, you can add what I call a pain-in-the-ass tax to the invoice. You add a solid 10% to 1000% to their bill to justify working with them.

For $100 an hour, I won't deal with much headache. For $1000 an hour, I can deal with quite a lot of headache. The beauty of the PIA tax is that often the headache client may clean up their act or just move along. Win-win indeed.

Tidbit 9: Leave your work at work and your life everywhere else.

Oftentimes, business owners do not shut off. They work all hours of the day, answer their phone on nights and weekends, and allow the business to interrupt their personal lives. This costs the business owner freedom and annoys his family and friends. It may even cost the business owner a relationship or two. I know plenty of business owners who ended up divorced, and it may be that the businesses they ran and how they ran those businesses became a contributing factor.

The key to keeping work and life separate is to set boundaries. You come in to work at a certain time and leave at a certain time. You do not work nights and weekends unless a special circumstance presents itself. Special circumstances cannot occur more than twice per month. Any work talk has to happen only when initiated by your spouse.

Rules like these are an example of keeping work where it belongs, packed away and not annoying you during your free, fun, and family time. (Though be sure to bring business cards wherever you go. Potential clients are lurking everywhere. Just be stealthy and brief so you can keep on living.)

> *"You just gotta keep livin' man, L-I-V-I-N."*
>
> -David Wooderson,
> played by Matthew McConaughey,
> in the movie *Dazed and Confused*

Some business owners claim they need to be on 24/7. No, my friend, you don't. Want a quick way to prove that? Step in the street and get hit by a bus. How many people that were going to call you in the next 72 hours will skip a beat in their lives because you're not available right this moment? My guess is not too many. You can train your clients to work around your rules. They learn to have rules for themselves as well. These boundaries make everyone happier.

Tidbit 10: Find a solution, not an excuse.

How many times have you had to give yourself a reason for not doing something, essentially rationalizing an emotional decision that may not have been the best? "I'm not going to cold call now, because no one is really at work today," or "They're probably busy, and I'd just be bugging them."

The solution in this case is to make the call, or take the action. You miss every shot you don't take, right? How will they get to buy your stuff if you don't tell them about and sell them your stuff?

> *"Don't find fault, find a remedy;*
> *anybody can complain."*
> -Henry Ford

Tidbit 11: Time is a commodity in short supply.

Don't waste it on things that don't make you a better person. Chill time is alright, in moderation. Though if you spend three hours a night chilling in front of the TV instead of growing, you'll find your business missing some vital flow.

Tidbit 12: Everybody's got to pit.

As a commodity, time is not something to take for granted. Every once in a while, you need to take a break. Maybe just a moment at a red light to reflect on all that you have accomplished or all that you've been given. Grab a fresh donut from that bakery you keep hearing about. Ask a buddy out for a beer. Take a vacation. Some down time is needed. But like everything else in business, remember that downtime is best in moderation.

Tidbit 13: Hang out with great people.

Imagine that you grew up homeless and poor in the inner

city. Your family was cruel and beat you. Every time you tried to grow or learn, someone did whatever they could to quell you. It's not that you couldn't advance in this circumstance, but you would have been at a decided disadvantage compared to someone who grew up in a more nurturing environment.

Now imagine you're an adult. (This shouldn't be too big of a stretch.) I want you to define what you want to be. Now I want you to look at who you hang out with routinely. Do they represent what you want to be? If they don't, it may be time for a new crowd. Life is short, and you become who you hang out with. Dirtballs, as they say, attract dirtballs.

> *"Who you spend time with is who you become! Change your life by consciously choosing to surround yourself with people with higher standards!"*
>
> -Tony Robbins

Tidbit 14: You cannot win a game without defined rules.

The analogy of business as a game is helpful. What are the rules of this game? Have you defined them? Whether the rules deal with ethics or your definition of success, it may be worth a few minutes to write down the top ten rules for your business. Start with what you must protect and how you look at money. Go from there and tweak as you see fit. These rules will become your code of conduct, so to speak, for your business. They help you make decisions when challenging times approach. Think of Google's rule: "Don't be evil."

Tidbit 15: Rules show up when principles do not align.

Nobody likes too many rules. They make it tough to play any game. You can find out what you can do with your company's rules to make sure that they align with the principals you want your company to have by filling in the blank: "We are at our best when…" Doing this will help your company maintain the character you want it to emulate and keep the rules realistic.

Tidbit 16: The seven-year itch applies to your business as well.

There will come a time in running your business when you will feel tired. You will feel worn out. You won't have as much fun as you did when you first got started. It happens to most business owners at one time or another. It even happens to employees. It definitely happens in relationships.

To navigate around this, remember why you started the whole venture. Does it bring you the juice for life that it once did? For many entrepreneurs, that once new and exciting business becomes just a job that sucks the life out of them, regardless of how much money they're making. This is why your reasons for running a business are so important.

> "My restless, roaming spirit would not allow me to remain at home very long."
> -Buffalo Bill

Because this is such a big issue and because you can cheat on your business a bit, your options to solve the seven-year itch are similar, if not more open, to relationship solutions. You will need to add some spice, some variety, some new products or services, or venture into new categories. Simply be aware what those actions will do to your existing business. Like some relationships, sometimes it's best to get out while you can and start something new. Have you ever been networking and heard someone say that they have been in the same business for 27 years or more? Is your first thought that they started a solid, exciting business? Or are you thinking that they must be the most boring person at a party? Or are they comfortable, which can lead to complacency?

What a deeper conversation will reveal is either someone screaming inside for change or a business person who has evolved their business enough to keep them interested.

Entrepreneurs are not at their best when they're idle. Keep your mind moving so that the seven-year itch does not creep in. If you keep it interesting, you will keep it moving and growing.

Tidbit 17: Have a space for your business.

This essentially means that regardless of what you do, you will need space to do it. Whether you rebuild engines, program apps, or day trade stocks, you need a space in which to do it. You need lots of space. More space than you initially think. The human mind perceives limitations in odd ways. Having a confined space can limit your creative self. Consider a church or lobby at a large office complex. Is there a practical reason for 30-foot high ceilings?

The solution is to create a space for you to run your business. Your cave, corner, desk, warehouse, stage, or workstation. You need a place where, when you get there, your mind knows it's go time.

> *"Don't underestimate the importance of having enough room to work. Grilling is much more relaxing when you are not trying to juggle a whole collection of plates and bowls as you do it. If your grill doesn't have enough workspace, and they almost never do, set up a table right next to your grill."*
>
> -Bobby Flay

Tidbit 18: Change is not only good, it is necessary.

You started your business with the intention to sell X, Y, and Z. Then X went out of style, Y became unnecessary, and Z simply had quality issues. Do you close up shop or do you adapt and start selling A, B, and C? Some companies do this very well. Others, such as all those Yellow Pages companies, are somewhat entertaining to watch as they flounder.

You need to evolve or die. Remember Kodak? After 124 years in business, they filed for bankruptcy in 2012. They refused to adapt to the changing landscape of their core business. Let's consider Amazon, a poster-child for evolution. People still read books, right? (I sure hope so.) Amazon started as a website that sold books. It sold $20,000 each week during its first two months of business. Still it lost over $300,000 that first year. Ouch! Then the company added toys, televisions, a portable electronic reader called the Kindle, and survived a few court challenges. It still failed to make much profit as it grew and began to define e-commerce. By 2014, Amazon accounted for roughly 60% of all books bought online. Now Amazon has become a major player in cloud computing and sells just about everything you could ever want to buy. The company has continued to evolve and grow. Though you could point to past profitability, in recent months, Amazon has made some cash. With a valuation of around $300 billion, and a reported 43% of all US e-commerce sales in 2016 going through them, they must be doing something right.

Evolution can often mean changing business names or logos. It can also mean you sell and start something new. The point is this: Never plateau. Never be complacent. Always be aware that new and different can offer opportunity that may quell your current business model. Don't be the guy stuck selling pagers to a few companies a year that had a booming business decades ago. Most things simply do not last without adaptation.

> *"It is not the strongest of the species that survives, nor the most intelligent: it is the one that is most adaptable to change."*
> -Charles Darwin, *Origin of Species*

Tidbit 19: Three meetings max

No more than three meetings with any single prospect. If, at the end of the third meeting, you don't have a clear yes, you obviously have a no from a person with more time than money. Let the potential client know your rule at the beginning of the second and third meetings. That way everyone understands that the others' time is valuable.

> *"Actions speak louder than meetings."*
> -Lee Clow

Tidbit 20: Never stop learning

At some point in your business career you may believe that you have seen it all. You probably haven't. Continue to attend classes and seminars, read until your eyes hurt and talk with people in business from all different backgrounds. It is amazing what you can learn chatting over coffee with someone you admire and having no objective other than picking their brain.

> *"Change is the end result of all true learning."*
> --Leo Buscaglia

We all learn from experience, even if at the time of the experience, we're unaware of what we are learning. For example, did you know that the more you trip, the better you are at not falling over when you do trip? Your brain takes the actions and reactions and creates a database of what works and what doesn't. This helps you survive, communicate, and live with either a lot of fear or a lot of fun, and maybe a few skinned knees when you were three years old.

> *"Education is the most powerful weapon you can use to change the world."*
> -Nelson Mandela

Whew! After all of these tidbits you should be set and solid with your business. These tidbits were learned by me the very hard way, so consider yourself enlightened a much easier way. Use only Tidbit #9 and you will be dramatically better than most business owners in living an enjoyable and stress free life.

Chapter 16

❝

"Am I shooting from the hip? Would any of this have happened if I was?"

-Taylor Swift

❞

This entire book was predicated on the conviction that you must do one crucial thing to have a bold business. It can be summed up in three words: Go for it.

Imagine that you started a business and you're doing pretty well. You find yourself on cruise control and you are happy with it. Then compare that with a life that involves challenging the status quo, kicking down every door, and looking for opportunities everywhere you go. You didn't start a business to chill on cruise control. You created a business to feed your drive as well as your hunger. Anyone can get a job. You chose to take a different path.

About six months before I ventured off on my own, I was offered a job with a company where a buddy of mine worked. I was in the process of getting my ducks in a row for my new business, keeping the lid on its release until it was time. My buddy knew I wasn't happy where I was, so he offered to have his boss interview me. I went to the interview, which was just a simple dinner at a nice restaurant. The man I met was nice enough, although there was something artificial about his personality. I took that meeting as a lesson of what I could become. I could take this job, make a little money, and be the daily grinder. Or I could venture off on my own and see what happens.

That meeting served as a test to see if I wanted to be a pawn or a player. Being a pawn offered a decent salary, paid vacation, and benefits. Being a player promised none of that. It did, however, offer the opportunity that no pawn can touch.

When I told my buddy that I wasn't interested in the job because I was about to go off and start my own gig, he seemed puzzled. It was only the second or third time that someone had challenged my decision to go off on my own. I've heard it dozens of times since then. I expect to hear it dozens more. You can expect to hear the same.

What have you got to lose?
What happens if you do nothing?
What happens if you start a business and fail to be bold?
Nothing. Or very little.

You need to decide to be bold and act on that decision. Just like the old riddle of the frogs. Five frogs were sitting on a log. One decided to jump off. How many frogs were still on the log? If you answered five, you understand the difference between deciding and acting.

I was reminded of this as I sat outside a fast-food restaurant one day. We often eat outside since we bring our dog with us anywhere we can. On that particular day, I was eating my food (the healthiest I could find on the menu, give or take), and I watched as car after car (or minivan after minivan) pulled up and waited for their food from the drive-through. Dozens of people, whose weight challenged the springs in their seats every day, were getting their 2000+ calorie meals delivered to them. It made me sad. I couldn't see how they were making themselves better.

> **"Freedom lies in being bold."**
> -Robert Frost

Boldness goes beyond business. Being bold can—and should—be a part of every facet of your life: your health, relationships, business, career, and hobbies. The people in the drive-through hadn't simply decided to give up one day. I presume most of them were doing the best they thought they could. The difference between the bold and the not-so-bold are the standards that they hold themselves to. They were content meeting the bare minimum that they found acceptable. You are, too. You just happen to have higher standards, which makes your bare minimum their dream.

This is one of the reasons people will question you and your bold business. You are breaking free to go beyond another person's or company's standards. You are rising above what many consider acceptable. You are driving a Ferrari that says BOSSMAN, while others cruise in their rusty Cavaliers. You take your millions and become the next Elon Musk, starting rocket ship companies, never satisfied and constantly improving. That is the way of the bold business owner.

Is this to say that a bold business person must be physically fit? Not necessarily. It is to say that if you are truly bold in one aspect of your life, you should shoot for being bold in other areas as well. That's what boldness is all about. And you don't become bold just for you. You make yourself bold for the entire world. You are making this world a better place because you exist.

Imagine if every bold business person that you knew opted against boldness. Can you imagine cell phones without

Steve Jobs? Cars without Henry Ford? Movies without Arnold Schwarzenegger? The world would be a different place without the bold doing what they do.

> ❝
> *When people said, "We never want to look like you." Arnold replied, "Don't worry. You never will."*
> -Arnold Schwarzenegger
> ❞

You can be one of those bold people. What will the world miss out on if you decide not to? The world has enough mundane people. You were provided with the tools and resourcefulness to be bold. It's time you showed a bit of appreciation by sharing your gift with the world. It's time for you to be bold. We will all thank you for using your gift.

What is the one action that you can take TODAY that will lead you to becoming more of a bold business owner?

> ❝
> *"In 1995 I had $7 bucks in my pocket and knew two things: I'm broke as hell and one day I won't be. You can achieve anything!"*
> -Dwayne 'The Rock' Johnson
> ❞

The Final Countdown

I want to thank you for checking out *The Bold Business Book*. The fact that you've read it means that you're well on your way to becoming a bold business owner. Without readers like you, my writing serves no purpose, so I want to sincerely thank you and say that I appreciate you taking the time to read this book. More importantly, I hope that you keep the pace of the bold business owner. If you've discovered some changes that may help your business, make them. Action trumps knowledge, every single time.

I am going to ask three things of you now that you are essentially done with this book:

What is with all of this bold talk?

1. Choose at least one thing that you are going to do in your business because of this book.
2. Email me at james@drawincustomers.com and let me know what that one thing is.
3. Share or gift this book to another potential bold business person.

Feel free to check out the Books for the Bold section I've included at the end of this book. I wouldn't know what I know without having taken action, and I wouldn't have taken those actions without having benefitted from the knowledge and insight shared by other visionaries.

If what you have read here has resonated with you, I and other business coaches are available to continue providing guidance at Draw In Customers Business Coaching. Whether you need a question answered, a simple session, or a long-term business coaching relationship to help you as you progress, we thrive on helping small businesses just like yours.

May the freedom and power of owning your own business give you the joy and success that you have worked so hard for. You have earned it, my fellow bold business owner!

The ART of good business is taking great action!

PS: Did you like the book? Leave a five star review and let the world know! ★★★★★

You Got This!

Now get to work.

Thanks!

To my wife for supporting me and tolerating me. To my kid for giving me something to work for. To my dog for trusting me to open the door for her. To my crew at Calls On Call for taking care of business while I was writing about it. To my clients at Draw In Customers Business Coaching: I have learned more from you than I ever taught you. To everyone I have ever had the pleasure of meeting, you have inspired me in some way or another, more than you know. To all of the authors of books everywhere, you keep the light of knowledge bright and flourishing. To the internet, you made the writing of this book possible in so many ways that I cannot imagine what writers did before.

To my wonderful editors:

Rachel Rasmussen
Trisha Alcisto
Tania Therien

Thank you a 1000x over for being so great. And I apologize for my many, many mistakes. You have all been a pleasure to work with and I wish you great success, freedom and fun in the future.

Thank you and good times!

Books for the Bold

I have read and listened to more books than I can count. I have been to presentations and sessions and have learned at least one thing from each of them. I'm going through three books at any given time. One upstairs, one downstairs, and one in my car to listen to as I cruise around to meetings and to the office. The library is just about the best deal that I've found. Check yours out today.

As a Man Thinketh
by James Allen

This is a quick read and arguably one of the best books on this list. It could change your life with its simple motto, "Calmness is power." What you think is who you are, so be wise to what you are thinking. Control your thoughts; do not be a result of them as if they were put in you by someone else. Fascinating and powerful.

Blink: The Power of Thinking Without Thinking
by Malcolm Gladwell

I really liked this book as an audiobook since it's the author who reads it. He adds emotion where it's needed. It covers the decision-making processes that go over our heads, ones we are typically not even aware of, mostly because we would take too long to decide what to do.

Book Yourself Solid
by Michael Port

Sometimes you just need a guidebook from someone that has a system for doing what you want done. Michael Port has such a guide. It has some great ideas, some great philosophies and some solid action steps for you to take.

Close the Deal: Smart Moves for Selling
by Sam Deep and Lyle Sussman

This book is a no-nonsense guide to sales spread out in an easy to digest format. An easy to use entry level sales guide.

Decisive: How to Make Better Choices in Life and Work
by Chip Heath and Dan Heath

To say Chip and Dan Heath have written some great books is an understatement. This book delves into the implicit systems in place as well as those that you can consciously use to make great decisions.

The Definitive Book of Body Language
by Alan Pease and Barbara Pease

Have you ever been in a meeting with someone whose signals didn't match what they were saying? Combine this book with Blink above and you'll be a powerful force in any meeting. It'll guide you to becoming more aware of the stances of others than they themselves may be.

Elements of Influence: The Art of Getting Others to Follow Your Lead
by Terry R. Bacon

Have you ever wondered at how someone else influenced you? What made you like them or do as they asked? You may benefit from becoming aware of what influences you and, more importantly, how you can influence others.

The Elements of Power: Lessons on Leadership and Influence
by Terry R. Bacon

In this book, Bacon goes through the elements of power to a degree of precision unlike most authors, even offering breakdowns of power in each element based on geography. He also gives you dos and don'ts for increasing power in each area. Fascinating book.

Emotional Intelligence: Why It Can Matter More Than IQ
by Daniel Goleman

This book has a foundation in science and is presented in a very interesting way. Stories are brought together along with dozens of studies to detail what it takes to be intelligent beyond just knowing some history or math. Emotional intelligence will probably take you further than typical book smarts ever will.

The E-Myth Revisited: Why Most Small Businesses Don't Work and What to Do About It
by Michael E Gerber

Michael Gerber takes the passion and hopes that many have for their business and challenges them with a simple question, Can you make this better, easier and make more money doing it? He answers this question with a simple, "Yes, with systems." Essentially, he tells you to get systems in place for everything in your business, regardless of size. It will scale much better.

Essentialism: The Disciplined Pursuit of Less
by Greg McKeown

We try to cram in so much stuff in our schedules, rooms, desks, houses, cars and minds that we often overburden ourselves unnecessarily. In this book, Greg argues that getting back to basics is the path to clarity. He's right.

The 4-Hour Workweek: Escape 9-5, Live Anywhere, and Join the New Rich (Expanded and Updated)
by Timothy Ferriss

Reading this book marked a turning point for me in my entrepreneurial career. It raised questions like: Why do you need to fill 40 hours a week with work? It really presents an outside-the-box way of looking at the actions that many business owners assume to be obligatory. What is holding you back may just be some old beliefs.

Frogs Into Princes
by Richard Bandler and John Grinder

Taken from a live conference from the founders of Neuro Linguistic Programming (NLP), this book uses NLP language to teach you how to use NLP. It is entertaining and thought provoking.

Games People Play: The Basic Handbook of Transactional Analysis.
by Eric Berne, M.D.

This is a sizable book that will constantly have you thinking of people you know who fit into each category. It's an older book that has withstood the test of time and continues to be an interesting read.

279

Good to Great: Why Some Companies Make the Leap...And Others Don't
by Jim Collins

Studying the difference between acceptable and insanely powerful is an exercise in best practices. You will reflect on your business time and again with this book.

The Hitchhiker's Guide to the Galaxy
by Douglas Adams

This is a fiction book that tells a story that applies to all of us in the real world. It tells a story in a manner that helps you define why you do what you do.

How to Connect in Business in 90 Seconds or Less
by Nicholas Boothman

This book is a crazy quick read. It provides a framework for getting your point across in seconds with more effect than you can even dream of doing in a one-hour speech. The power is in brevity.

How to Win Friends & Influence People
by Dale Carnegie

This book essentially states the obvious: Be nice and take care of others, and the rest will fall into place. As is often the case with good books, its stories are entertaining while its lessons are instructive. Decades later, it's still a strong addition to any personal library.

Influence: The Psychology of Persuasion
by Robert Cialdini

Have you ever left the scene of a purchase and thought, what just happened? This book outlines seven basic principles for how we can and do influence people. It is entertaining, straightforward and genius.

Jack: Straight from the Gut
by Jack Welch

The guy has a very strong personality and has his lovers and haters. But you cannot argue with the success GE enjoyed while he was around. His straight talk is welcome. The man did alright, and he can teach you a thing or two.

The New One Minute Manager
by Ken Blanchard and Spencer Johnson

This book goes about educating you on how to connect with your employees quickly. Managing more than a few minutes a day is not ideal. You need speed and agility in this field, and this book helps you get it.

Oh, the Places You'll Go!
by Dr. Suess

Yeah, I included a Dr. Suess book. This book is necessary reading for toddlers as well as new business owners. Few books offer the insight and motivation that this book packs into a kids book.

One Simple Idea
by Stephen Key

We have all had an idea for a product that would be a phenomenal invention. Most of us do not act on these ideas because we really don't know what the next steps are. This book outlines the basics.

The One Thing
by Gary Keller with Jay Papasan

How often have you realized you have way too many things going on and it is tough to complete even marginal tasks? This book is a book that teaches you to focus on one thing.

The Power of Habit: Why We Do What We Do in Life and Business
by Charles Duhigg

This book puts into perspective what you and others do each day with little to no thought. From brand loyalty to routines before bed, this book will have you thinking about your every action. Great book to combine with Blink.

Priceless
by William Poundstone

How do you price your product or service? How do you know what people will pay? I was going to price this book at $649 until I was told that was probably too much. This book outlines how the book you are holding is a steal.

The Sandler Rules: 49 Timeless Selling Principles and How to Apply Them
by David Mattson

This book shares 49 sales rules to follow. Nothing about the customer being right. More along the lines of you deserving sales because you do sales. You are awesome. Now pick up the phone and prove it.

The Secret Handshake
by Kathleen Kelly Reardon

This book details a lot of inner-circle politics in big business. Though it concentrates on large corporations and the maneuvering that happens within them, it does apply to your small business and the deal-making you will need to do with vendors and employees.

The 7 Habits of Highly Effective People: Powerful Lessons in Personal Change
by Stephen R. Covey

This recommendation goes without saying as it is one of the most celebrated books ever written for business. Entire classes have been dedicated to studying the principles in this book. A must read.

Social Intelligence: The New Science of Human Relationships
by Daniel Goleman

This was written by the author of Emotional Intelligence. It explores yet another side of intelligence that has not been researched as much as your typical brain-dump tests. Very interesting book.

The Talent Code: Greatness Isn't Born. It's Grown. Here's How
by Daniel Coyle

This book explores the skills of top performers by researching myelin inside the brain. Continued practice can increase the myelin inside your brain for certain nerve cells, making complex actions simple.

Talent IQ: Identify Your Company's Top Performers, Improve or Remove Underachievers, Boost Productivity and Profit
by Emmett C Murphy

This is a book on finding the right people. When I first started my business, I thought employees were the easy part. Spoiler alert: They are not.

Talent is Overrated: What Really Separates World-Class Performers from Everybody Else
by Geoff Colvin

Many people will see a skilled artist or performer and look in awe and wonder. That's great until you realize that you have the ability to learn and train to do great things. It just takes a lot of practice.

The 10X Rule: The Only Difference Between Success and Failure
by Grant Cardone

This guy is amazing to watch. A little on the abrasive side for many, but so am I. He offers a no-nonsense approach to getting better return on your work by working harder and smarter. An interesting counter argument to The 4-Hour Workweek.

The Tipping Point: How Little Things Can Make a Big Difference
by Malcolm Gladwell

Another great book by Malcolm Gladwell. It also touches on the brain and decision-making and the power inside that cranium of yours.

Traction
by Gabriel Weinberg and Justin Mares

This book touches on many of the opportunities you have for marketing your brand and finding what works and what does not. Then making moves to increase your efforts in the channels that work.

You Can't Teach a Kid to Ride a Bike at a Seminar: The Sandler Sales Institute's 7-Step System for Successful Selling
by David H. Sandler

I have been through years of Sandler training and have been impressed with most of his teachings. He was a no-nonsense type of guy that told it to you straight. Hence the title.

You Got This! A Motivational Guide for Achieving Your Goals
by James Kademan

Yes, that James Kademan. This is the book to have for motivation. It is literally filled with over 200 pages of huge print that states clearly, "You Got This!" It follows up with a plan to focus that motivation by telling you to get to work.

Wear Sunscreen: A Primer for Real Life
by Mary Schmich
    A very short book that is essentially a poem with timeless advice.

What Every BODY is Saying: An Ex-FBI Agent's Guide to Speed-Reading People
by Joe Navarro
    Nonverbal communication tells you the real story much better than the words people tell you. This book details some of the cues and motions to look for as you communicate with people.

What the Dog Saw
by Malcolm Gladwell
    This book really illustrates the essence of perspective. That is to say, your experience and my experience of the same event may be different. Touching on the perspectives of case studies like Ronco, this book opens up your eyes to what others may see.

Who
by Geoff Smart and Randy Street
    Employees can be a tough challenge. Having a system to hire, motivate and fire employees is a must. These HR masters layout some fantastic ideas as well as surprising interview questions to use in your hiring process.

Winning
by Jack Welch
    This book from the former CEO of GE is a testament to the juggernaut of a company that Welch ran. It speaks to companies of all sizes and gives you a closer look into what made Jack tick.

Zero to One
by Peter Thiel
    This book subscribes to the notion that if you are not going to change the world with your business, why start a business?

Draw In Customers

Business Coaching

Draw In Customers Business Coaching specializes in helping small business owners grow in profitability and free time as well as helping them find ways to have more fun in their business. The small businesses they serve range from startups to well-established companies. They specialize in working with service businesses with less than 30 employees.

If you know of a company that has been stagnant for too long and could use a boost, a free business coaching session with Draw In Customers may be all that's needed. Call (608) 210-2221 or email *coach@drawincustomers.com*.

FREE Business Coaching Session

Schedule your free business coaching session at
https://drawincustomers.com/free

CALLS ON CALL

Calls On Call Shared Receptionist Service offers small business owners a way to get back the freedom and flexibility that they started their business for in the first place by removing the burden of having to be available constantly to answer their phones. Calls On Call takes care of incoming as well as outgoing phone calls, emails, and calendars for small businesses ranging from massage therapists to electricians to IT companies.

With a dedicated Calls On Call receptionist, your clients will not know that you are saving money as you offer the excellent customer service that only a company like Calls On Call can offer. Missed calls mean missed profit. Calls On Call is the solution to getting every call answered and being free to enjoy your life as an entrepreneur.

FREE Phone Answering Setup*
($600 value)

Call (608)210-3110 or email *hello@callsoncall.com* for more information.

must mention this book.

About the Author

James Kademan resides in Madison, Wisconsin with his wife, son, and loving dog. He owns Calls On Call, a shared receptionist company, and Draw In Customers Business Coaching, a company that supports small businesses in growth, profitability, and eventual exit.

James volunteers with Big Brothers Big Sisters, sits on many boards, speaks about small business startup and growth to many organizations, and helps entrepreneurs from all walks of life as often as he can.

He studies neuro-linguistic programming and strategic intervention through Robbins-Madanes Training designed by Tony Robbins and Cloe Madanes.

James continues to write books and blog all over the internet. When he isn't talking or learning about business, he can be found driving or flying faster than he should on his way to speak about business.

James can be reached at *james@drawincustomers.com* or by calling (608) 210-2221.